Light the Candles!

Songs of praise and ceremony from around the world

Compiled by
June B. Tillman

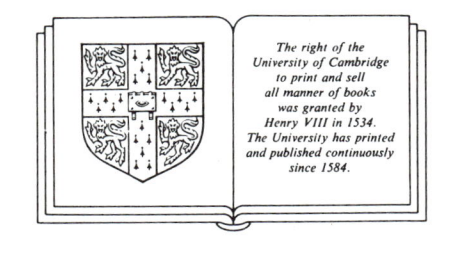

Cambridge University Press

Cambridge

New York   Port Chester   Melbourne   Sydney

Song books and musical activity books published by Cambridge University Press

Seasonal Songs by Dot Paxton
A collection of easy-to-learn songs for each season of the year with ideas for 'spin-off' work
ISBN 0 521 33668 6

The Christmas Search
A pageant of carols, narrative and rhyme, compiled by June Tillman
ISBN 0 521 33968 5

Story, song and dance
For the young, a collection of ideas for improvised drama with music, compiled by Jean Gilbert
Book   ISBN 0 521 33967 7
Cassette   ISBN 0 521 32758 X

Music through topics by Veronica Clark
An activity resource book and cassette for teachers of 4 to 8 year-olds
Book   ISBN 0 521 34842 0
Cassette   ISBN 0 521 35630 X

Light the Candles!
Songs of praise and ceremony from around the world, compiled by June Tillman
ISBN 0 521 33969 3

Titles in the *Cambridge Young Musicals* series

The Bells of Lyonesse
ISBN 0 521 33590 6

Seaspell
Piano/Conductor edition   ISBN 0 521 33588 4
Performers' edition   ISBN 0 521 33589 2

Duffy and the devil
Piano/Conductor edition   ISBN 0 521 33592 2
Performers' edition   ISBN 0 521 33593 0

African Madonna
Piano/Conductor edition   ISBN 0 521 37880 X
Performers' edition   ISBN 0 521 39811 8

Useful additional resource material
Themes in World Religions
Vol. 1   ISBN 0 521 35584 2
Vol. 2   ISBN 0 521 35585 0

Published by the Press Syndicate of the University of Cambridge
The Pitt Building, Trumpington Street, Cambridge CB2 1RP
40 West 20th Street, New York, NY 10011, USA
10 Stamford Road, Oakleigh, Melbourne 3166, Australia

© Cambridge University Press 1991

First published 1991

Printed in Great Britain by Bell and Bain Ltd, Glasgow

British Library cataloguing in publication data
Tillman, June B.
  Light the candles!: songs of praise and ceremony from around the world.
  1. Songs in English – Collections
  I. Title
  784.3'06

ISBN 0 521 33969 3

Illustrations by Frané Lessac
Cover illustration by Frané Lessac

ME

Light the Candles!
Songs of Praise and Ceremony from around the World

This collection of songs from many parts of the world is designed to be sung by groups of children from a variety of religions both in schools and wherever different faiths worship together.

The songs are grouped into four sections:
- Festivals and Seasons
- Special Events
- One World
- Songs of Praise

Each section gives details of
- the time of year appropriate to each song
- the type of event being celebrated
- the origin of each song

In compiling this collection the author has used many sources:
- material already published
- material produced by local education authorities
- music from recordings of schools, individuals and communities

It is hoped that *Light the Candles!* will bring new cultures alive, so that all faiths can join together in Songs of Praise and Ceremony.

Publisher's acknowledgements

Many of the songs in this book are in copyright. For details, please refer first to the page on which the song appears.

If application is made in writing, the Permissions Controller of Cambridge University Press will endeavour to forward correspondence regarding permissions to private individuals. The following is a list of songs which are in the copyright of publishers and other institutions. They may be contacted direct.

Every effort has been made to reach copyright holders. The publishers would be glad to hear from anyone whose rights they have unknowingly infringed.

5 On the first Thanksgiving Day
A traditional North American song. Arranged by Theron Haithwaite. © 1985 Silver Burdett Company. Used by permission. Silver Burdett & Ginn, Simon & Schuster School Group, 250 James Street, Morristown, New Jersey, USA.

6 Cheshire souling song
A traditional English song. From *Autumn*, eds Adams, Leach and Palmer, published by Blackie and Son Ltd, Bishopriggs, Glasgow G64 2NZ.

12 Matsukazari *Japanese New Year's song*
Arrangement of a traditional Japanese song. Translated by Rosemary Jacques. © 1985 Silver Burdett Company. Used by permission. Silver Burdett & Ginn, Simon & Schuster School Group, 250 James Street, Morristown, New Jersey, USA.

14 Chinese lantern song
Text translated by Stephen Jones, melody and arrangement by Kenneth Pont. From *The Lantern Song Book*, © Oxford University Press, reproduced by permission.

16 Cân y grempog *The pancake song*
A traditional Welsh song. Translated by O. Griffiths and Roy Palmer. From *Caneuon Llafar Gwlad (Songs from Oral Tradition)*, editor D. Roy Saer, © National Museum of Wales – Welsh Folk Museum, 1974. Amgueddfa Werin Cymru, Sain Ffagan, Caerdydd CF5 6XB.

17 Great is His love
Music by Joseph Gelineau. Published by The Grail (England), 125 Waxwell Lane, Pinner, Middlesex HA5 3ER.

18 Whey he day?
Words and music by Anthony Pierre, © 1980 McCrimmon Publishing Co. Ltd, 10–12 High Street, Great Wakering, Essex SS3 0EQ.

19 Arnaki ke likos *The lamb and the wolf*
A Greek folk song collected from Maria Roussou, translated by Nitsa Sergides, English lyrics and accompaniment by Jean Gilbert. From *Festivals* by Jean Gilbert, © Oxford University Press.

20 H'ristos anesti *Jesus has risen*
A Greek Easter hymn, translated by Nitsa Sergides. English words by Jean Gilbert. From *Festivals* by Jean Gilbert, © Oxford University Press.

21 The Son of God
Words and music by Cynthia Allen. © 1980 McCrimmon Publishing Co. Ltd, 10–12 High Street, Great Wakering, Essex SS3 0EQ.

30 Lord of all hopefulness
Words by Jan Struther (1901–53) from *Enlarged Songs of Praise*, reprinted by permission of Oxford University Press. Music traditional Irish, arranged by June Tillman.

36 Still now
A traditional Inuit song, arranged by June Tillman. From 'Eskimo Lullaby', English translation by Edith Fulton Fowke, © 1954 Waterloo Music Co. Ltd, Waterloo, Ontario, all rights reserved, used by permission.

42 One world
Words and music by R.W. Tysoe. Reproduced by permission of Stainer & Bell Ltd, PO Box 110, 82 High Road, London N2 9PW.

46 Buddhist blessings
Words by Koddaka-Patha and Sutta Nipa, adapted by Colin Hodgetts. Music by Colin Hodgetts. Reproduced by permission of Stainer & Bell Ltd, PO Box 110, 82 High Road, London N2 9PW.

56 Ogun ba mi re *Song to Ogun*
and

57 Onisango
Both are traditional Yoruba songs, collected by Anthony King. From *Yoruba Sacred Music from Ekiti* by Anthony King. Published by Ibadan University Press, Nigeria.

58 Ruaumoko
Words by Ratu Tibble, adapted by June Tillman. Music by Sam Freedman. Published by Viking Sevenseas Ltd, PO Box 152, Paraparaumu, New Zealand.

63 Carol of the creatures
Words and music by Sydney Carter. Reproduced by permission of Stainer & Bell Ltd, PO Box 110, 82 High Road, London N2 9PW.

64 By the rivers of Babylon
Traditional, adapted by Dowe and McNaughton. Published by A & C Black (Publishers) Ltd, Howard Road, Eaton Socon, Cambs PE19 3EZ.

65 De angels rejoicin'
A traditional Caribbean song. From *Songs from Trinidad*, collected by Edric Connor, © Oxford University Press.

67 The bell of creation
Words and music by Sydney Carter. Reproduced by permission of Stainer & Bell Ltd, PO Box 110, 82 High Road, London N2 9PW.

Contents

Author's preface

Festivals and Seasons

1	Tapuchim ud' vash *Apples and honey*	8
2	I'm building a sukkah	10
3	Are bhalo *A jari for harvest*	12
4	Village festival	15
5	On the first Thanksgiving Day	16
6	Cheshire souling song	18
7	A happy time	20
8	Oh Chanukah	22
9	Munji Aziz ka jnumdin *Jesus's birth*	24
10	Charni may bahar *Joy in the manger*	26
11	Master Hee-haw	28
12	Matsukazari *Japanese New Year's song*	30
13	Chinese New Year	32
14	Chinese lantern song	34
15	My name is Purim	36
16	Cân y grempog *The pancake song*	38
17	Great is His love	39
18	Whey he day?	42
19	Arnaki ke likos *The lamb and the wolf*	44
20	H'ristos anesti *Jesus has risen*	46
21	The Son of God	48
22	Holi with Shyam	50
23	Phagun lege *Spring song*	52
24	Padstow May Day song	54
25	John Barleycorn	56
26	Buddha Lord we offer *Holy day of Wesak*	58
27	Avare varsad *Come, come, rain*	60
28	Aye re aye *Eid is here*	60
29	Eid ul-Bukr	62

Special Events

30	Lord of all hopefulness	64
31	Jabbin, Jabbin *Rise! Rise!*	65
32	Shabbat shalom	66
33	Hoya-hoye *We'll come again*	68
34	Kalo sile *Come, let us go*	70
35	Salani *Farewell song*	71
36	Still now	72
37	Somagwaza *Initiation song*	74
38	Hey Motswala	76
39	Arabic wedding chant	78
40	Allah ju main *I am all alone*	79
41	A Lyke Wake dirge	80

One World

42	One world	82
43	The world is dark	84
44	Ɔdɔ N'Eye *Love your neighbour*	87
45	Nkosi sikelel'i Afrika *Bless our country*	88
46	Buddhist blessings	90
47	Like a beautiful journey	92

Songs of Praise

48	Simple gifts	94
49	Hevenu shalom *Peace unto you*	96
50	Raghupati *Gandhi's favourite hymn*	97
51	Into the future	98
52	Jon, jané, jana	100
53	Koee bolay Ram Ram *Some do call you Rama*	102
54	Sanctus	105
55	Ruu tat *The heavens are speaking*	106
56	Ogun ba mi re *Song to Ogun*	107
57	Onisango	108
58	Ruaumoko	109
59	Twameva *You are my mother*	112
60	Shri Ram *Lord Ram*	113
61	Hare Krishna *Praise Lord Krishna*	114
62	Let us praise Him	115
63	Carol of the creatures	116
64	By the rivers of Babylon	118
65	De angels rejoicin'	121
66	A child's prayer	122
67	The bell of creation	124

Index of song titles 127

Index of first lines (in English) 128

Author's preface

The production of this book has proved to be a challenging, exciting and difficult task. There were moments of great joy, but many problems were encountered and these I may have solved with a greater or lesser degree of success. This preface is an attempt to share with the user some of these problems.

The greatest problem was the wide diversity of languages. Most of these were unfamiliar to me and also to those involved in the publication and, although every attempt has been made to check the accuracy at each stage in publication, I apologise for any errors that may have slipped in. Many of the languages do not use the West European ('Roman') alphabet, so the first task was to transcribe them phonetically. There is in the present state of inter-cultural dialogue no standard transliteration into the Western alphabet and therefore material in the same language collected from two different sources may not necessarily be consistent, although every effort has been made to make it so. Some sounds were almost impossible to represent. The next stage was to find out the meaning of the song from the contributor and produce a singable version. As this task was complex, I have not made any attempt at rhyme. There is a school of thought that would recommend songs from non-British traditions to be sung in their original language. I, however, felt it best to offer teachers as many choices as possible. If the musical idiom is unfamiliar to pupils and they are also asked to cope with an unfamiliar language, the song may be rejected as too difficult. Some teachers, therefore, may prefer to introduce the song in English and use the original language at a later stage.

As many of the sources were oral and notated from tape-recordings, various elements characteristic of the oral process of transmission can be observed. In some songs, for example 'Allah ju main', verses have got lost; in other cases users may know different versions of the songs. One of the problems of collecting from children was that, if they spoke a number of languages, they got the words confused, producing in some cases curiously hybrid songs. Most of these problems have, I hope, now been sorted out. Because of the method of collecting, it has clearly been difficult to trace with any certainty the owners of the copyright of some of the material. I apologise for any errors in this area and trust they can be corrected in later editions.

Not only are some of the songs in unfamiliar languages, but their musical idiom is different from that for which traditional West European classical notation was designed. It is difficult, for example, to capture the subtleties of vocal ornamentation in some of the Asian material. Tapes of a variety of musical idioms are available at the University of London Institute of Education, collected as part of a research project initiated by the EEC. I hope that the collection will also inspire people to invite performers from other traditions to give live performances.

There has been an attempt to keep a balance between traditions from all over the world, but I had to collect what was actually available. Some traditions seem to sing more than others and, in some parts of the world, religious songs are not considered to be appropriate. There are no examples in this book of chanting, which is common in some religious traditions. This is because of the difficulty in notating them and retaining their spirit.

With such a wide variety of traditions represented, it is inevitable that some people will find some material easily accessible and popular, while other songs may appear strange, unfamiliar and difficult. I hope that users will none the less persevere with the less easy songs. 'Shri Ram', for example, is a good starting-point for the material from the Indian subcontinent.

It is difficult to name all the people who have helped me on the journey that has led to this book. The names of many are on the songs themselves. Others who offered help and encouragement are R.T. Abrams, John Blacking, the Buddhist Society, Gordon Cox, Brian Cryer, John Ferguson, the Japanese Embassy, the Jewish Education Bureau, Ranjit Kalsi, Anthony Ogg, Brian Pearce, Arunthaty Srikantha Rajah, Leela Ramdeen, Tilak Shankar, and the staff and pupils of Furzedown Primary School. The project has resulted in many new friendships. I hope that this collection will bring new cultures alive for others, too.

June B. Tillman

Festivals and Seasons

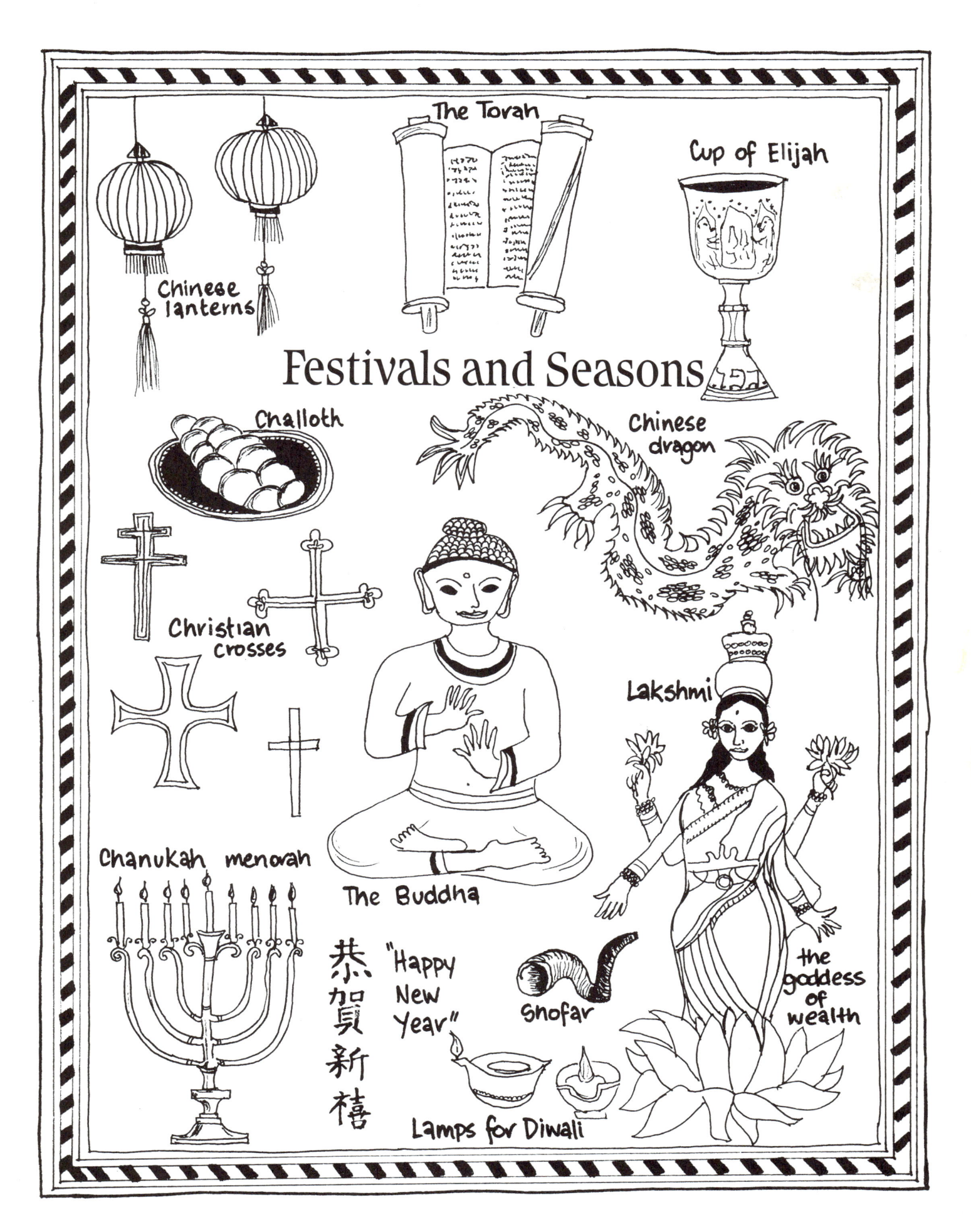

- Chinese lanterns
- The Torah
- Cup of Elijah
- Challoth
- Chinese dragon
- Christian crosses
- The Buddha
- Lakshmi, the goddess of wealth
- Chanukah menorah
- 恭賀新禧 "Happy New Year"
- Shofar
- Lamps for Diwali

1 Tapuchim ud' vash
Apples and honey

Traditional Jewish

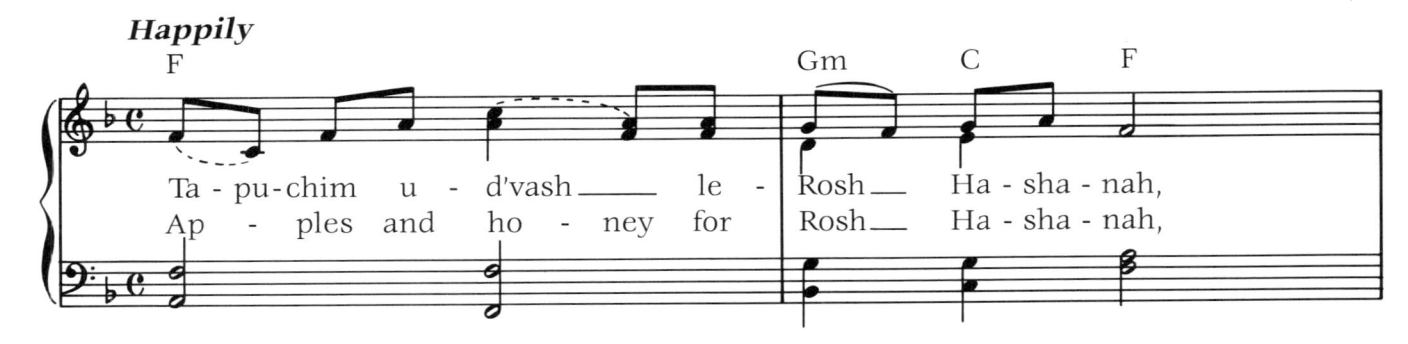

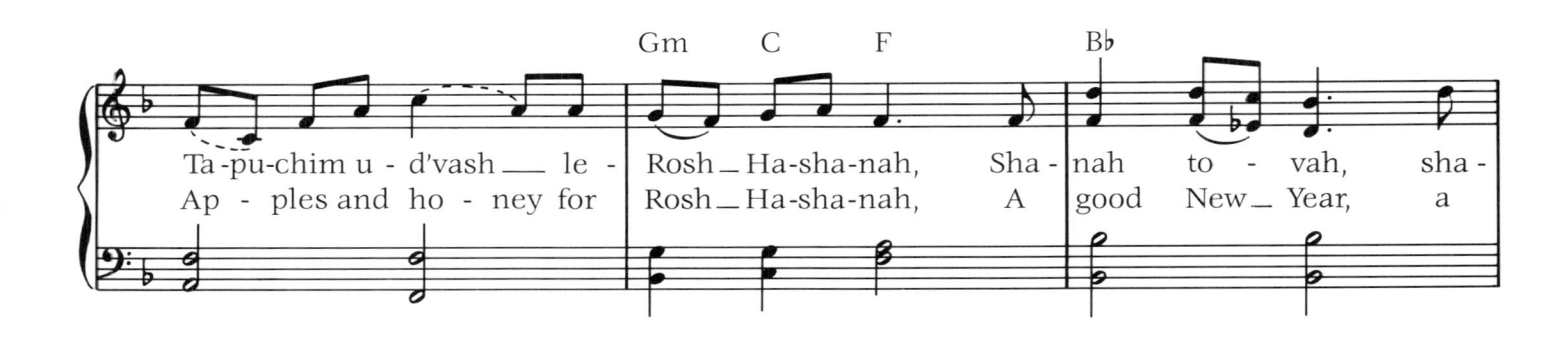

Happily

Ta-pu-chim u-d'vash le-Rosh Ha-sha-nah,
Ap-ples and ho-ney for Rosh Ha-sha-nah,

Ta-pu-chim u-d'vash le-Rosh Ha-sha-nah, Sha-nah to-vah, sha-
Ap-ples and ho-ney for Rosh Ha-sha-nah, A good New Year, a

nah me-tu-kah! Ta-pu-chim u-d'vash le-Rosh Ha-sha-nah.
sweet New Year! Ap-ples and ho-ney for Rosh Ha-sha-nah.

Rosh Hashanah

Rosh Hashanah is the Jewish New Year celebration. It falls in the autumn, although the first month of the Jewish calendar is in the springtime, and marks the instruction in the Torah, or Jewish holy book: 'On the first day of the seventh month you shall not do any work. You shall celebrate and sound the shofar.'

Jews look backward and forward at Rosh Hashanah. Sometimes it is called the Day of Remembering, when God thinks about the world he has created, or the Day of Judgement, when God remembers the deeds of all people and judges the world for the coming year.

It is also called the Day of Blowing the Shofar, an instrument made from the curved horn of a ram or goat. The shofar is sounded in the synagogue to mark the beginning of the Holy Days, to remind Jews of God the ruler and judge and to warn them to improve their ways.

In the afternoon, families gather on the banks of a river, lake or pond to recite prayers asking for forgiveness. Then they shake out the dust from their pockets or throw breadcrumbs into the water as if they were getting rid of their sins.

The period of ten Holy Days called the Ten Days of Forgiveness, a time for self-examination, ends with Yom Kippur, the Day of Atonement. Although Rosh Hashanah is a serious festival, there is also merrymaking; cards are sent, candles are lit and prayers recited. *Challoth*, twisted loaves, sometimes with a braided crown to remind people of the kingship of God, are eaten, along with apples dipped in honey to signify sweetness in the coming year.

2 I'm building a sukkah

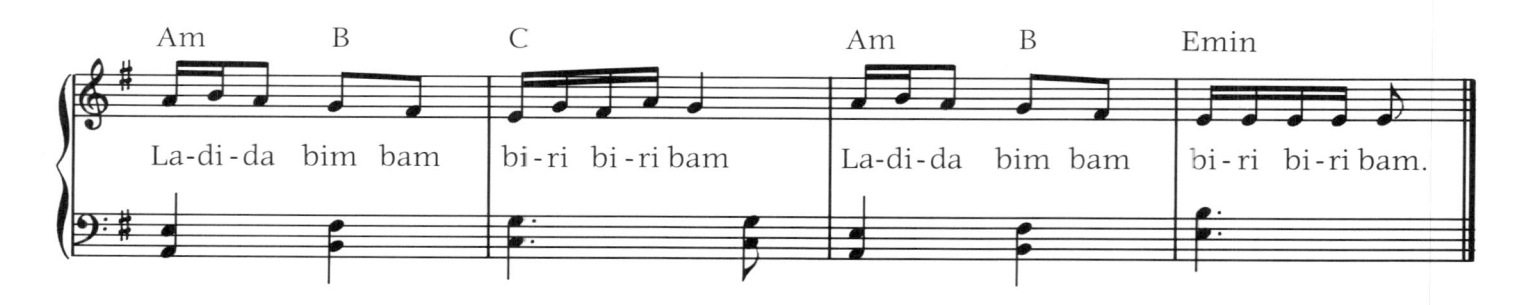

Traditional Jewish

Steadily

1. I'm building a sukkah, My hammer doesn't stop, La-di-da bim bam bi-ri bi-ri bam Oh bring me the schach for I've reached the ve-ry top! La-di-da bim bam bi-ri bi-ri bam La-di-da bim bam bi-ri bi-ri bam.

2. I'll sit in the Sukkah like Noah in the Ark,
   La-di-da, etc.

   I'll drink and be merry from morning to dark!
   La-di-da, etc.

3. Come friends and neighbours, come right along,
   La-di-da, etc.

   Join us in eating and singing a song,
   La-di-da, etc.

Festivals and Seasons

Pitched Percussion

Descant Recorders

Sukkoth

Sukkoth, the Jewish harvest festival, falls at the time of the grape harvest. Also called the Festival of Tabernacles or Booths, it fulfils the instruction in the Torah (the first section of the Jewish holy book): 'You shall live in booths for seven days, so you may remember that the Jewish people lived in booths when they were freed from slavery in Egypt.'

Some people decorate their homes with branches, but others make a booth or sukkah in their garden from leaves and branches. The roof (*schach*) is the most important part of the sukkah; it must be made of things that grow, and be open to the sky. The sukkah reminds people of the shelters that Jewish people built in the desert on their journey to escape from slavery in Egypt. It also resembles the huts that farmers used to build in the fields so that they could harvest their crops speedily. Sukkoth used to be a time of pilgrimage to Jerusalem and pilgrims used to build shelters in courtyards and on roof tops.

In the synagogue, symbolic branches of palm, myrtle, willow and *etrog* (the fruit of the citron tree) are waved in all directions to show that God is everywhere. The festival lasts eight days, with the first and last being days of rest, and a family may live in their sukkah for this time. On the last day prayers are offered for rain, and the old temple ceremony of drawing water is remembered. Rain is particularly important in Israel because the summer is completely dry and rabbis used to say that at Sukkoth God decides how much rain will fall in the coming year.

Festivals and Seasons

3 Are bhalo
A jari for harvest

Traditional Bengali
Translated by S. Mitra and June Tillman

Steadily

A - re bha - lo bha - lo ____ bha - lo re bhai, A - re oh ____ a - ha ____ be - sh bhai, Am-ra nai - cha nai - cha ____ sa - bai jai. Am-ra nai - cha nai - cha ____ sa - bai jai. Sho - no ka - n sho - no ka - n mo - mi - n bhai, Am - ra be - a ____ da pir ____ map - ti chai.

Is all well ____ with you, ____ bro-ther? Is it all well? Is it all ____ ga - thered ____ in ____ now? We are dan - cing, dan - cing at har - vest time. We are dan - cing, dan - cing at har - vest time. Bro-ther, do you not hear now the mu - sic that plays? Leave your sor - rows ____ far be - hind you now.

Shouted

Ti - le - te to - i - l hai, Du - d - he hai doi! Dha - ne - te to - i - ar hai! Mu - ri chi - ra khoi, A - re be - sh be - sh be - sh bhai.

Milk gives us ve - ry great strength, ve - ry great strength, yes! Corn is the staff of our life! Now it's har - vest - ed. All is ga - thered, ga - thered, ga - thered in.

Festivals and Seasons

Sa-bash sa-bash sa-bash bhai, Sa-bash sa-bash sa-bash go, Be-sh be-sh
Har-vest, har-vest, har-vest time. Ga-thered, ga-thered, ga-thered in, Har-vest, har-vest

go. Sa-bash go be-sh go be-sh go sa-bash go
time. Ga-thered in, har-vest time, ga-thered in, har-vest time,

Sung

A - re oh phu-ler bha - re go bha - re.
See the fields are all filled now with glow-ing flowers.

Phu - ler bha - re dal pa - re a - li - a.
Flo - wers now are bloom - ing ev' - ry - where.

Ni-sha ka-le pho-to phul Ni - hur la - gi - a.
We can go and ga-ther arm-fuls as we sing our song now.

Bhra - ra - mo - ra na ka - re ra - ma - du - ro la - gi - a -
Lis-ten to the bees as they ga - ther ho - ney from the

re. Eh eh phu-ler bha - re go bha - re.
flow'rs. See the fields are all filled now with glowing flow'rs.

Phu - ler bha - re dal pa - re a - li - a.
Flo - wers now are bloo - ming ev' - ry - where.

• Festivals and Seasons 13

Bhai-er sha-ke Jan di-bo Ga-lai di-bo chu-ri.
All our bro-thers have spent their time get-ting in the har-vest.

Bhra-mo-ra na ka-re ra ma-du-ro la-gi-a-
Lis-ten to the bees as they ga-ther ho-ney from the

re. Eh eh phu-ler bha-re go bha-re phu-ler ba-re
flow'rs. See the fields are all filled now with glowing flowers. Flo-wers now are

dal pa-re a-li-a. Ban-da-na sha-ri-a mo-ra
bloo-ming ev'-ry-where. When we've fi-nished wor-ship-ping we'll

Gai-bo jar-i-r gan Kar-ba-la ka-hi-nir duk-he bi-da-re pa-ram.
sing our ja-ri song. Join with me to sing it now and praise the har-vest home.

This song from Bengal is a *jari* – a song of thanksgiving at harvest time. It is usually sung by men – Hindus and Muslims together – at the end of a hard day's work in the rice fields. Rice is the staple food in this region of India. The song gives thanks for milk that nourishes life, and for a good harvest, and is sung to the accompaniment of a drum.

4 Village festival

Traditional Japanese

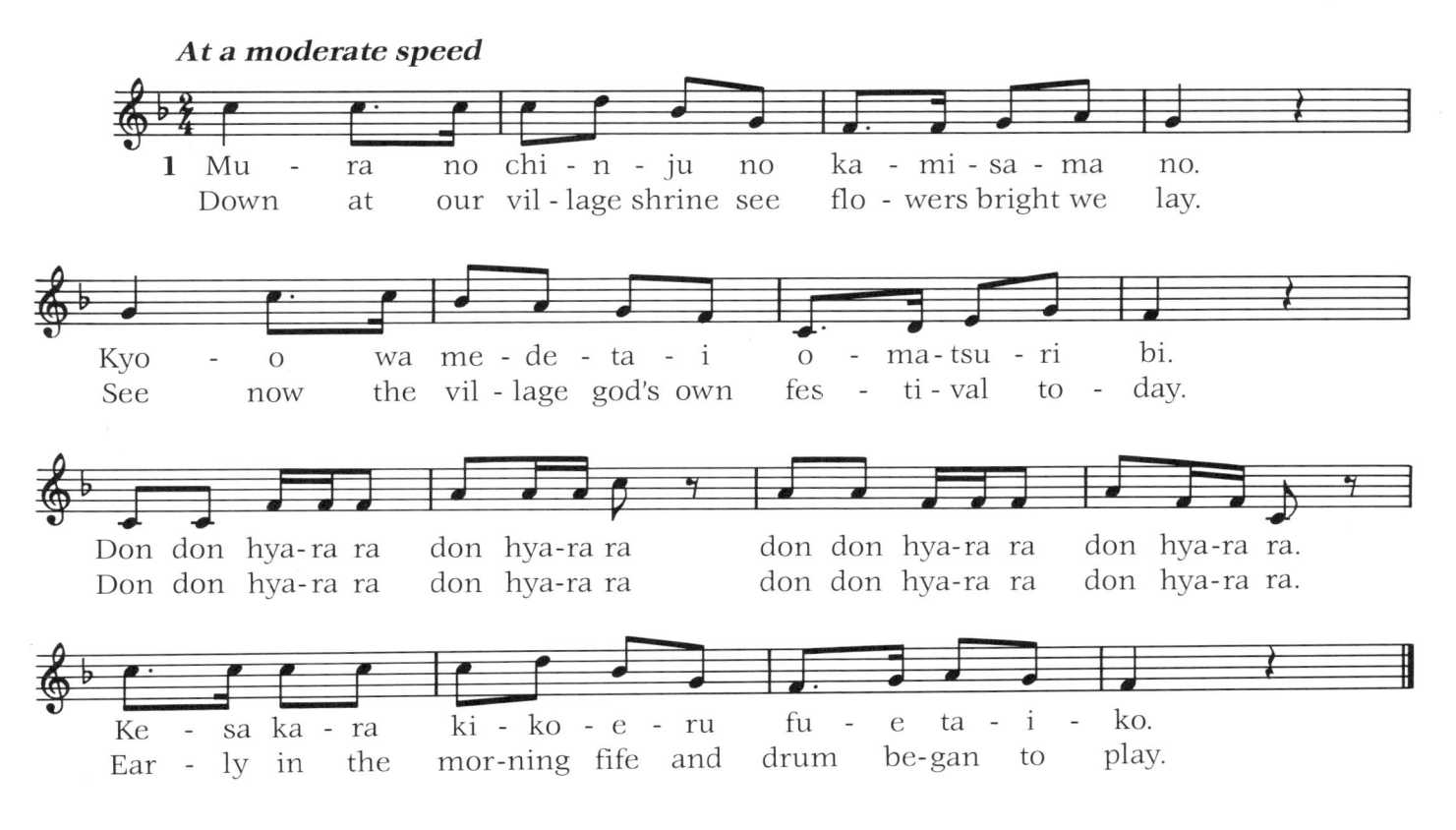

At a moderate speed

1. Mu - ra   no   chi - n - ju   no   ka - mi - sa - ma   no.
   Down   at   our vil - lage shrine see   flo - wers bright we   lay.

   Kyo - o   wa me - de - ta - i   o - ma - tsu - ri   bi.
   See   now   the vil - lage god's own   fes - ti - val to - day.

   Don don hya - ra ra   don hya - ra ra   don don hya - ra ra   don hya - ra ra.
   Don don hya - ra ra   don hya - ra ra   don don hya - ra ra   don hya - ra ra.

   Ke - sa ka - ra   ki - ko - e - ru   fu - e ta - i - ko.
   Ear - ly in the   mor - ning fife and   drum be - gan to   play.

2. This was a year of plenty and the rice abounds.
   All in the town are joyful, hear the festive sounds;
   Don don hyara ra, don hyara ra,
   Don don hyara ra, don hyara ra.
   Till it's late see things are bustling in the temple grounds.

Add a finger cymbal on the first beat of each bar. Pronounce 'i' as in **ink** *and 'e' as in* **egg**.

Japanese festivals

Although there are many Buddhist temples in Japan, the state religion is Shinto and each village and town has its shinto shrine. Shintoism believes in a vast number of gods known as *Kami*. The chief among these is the sun-goddess, whose son is married to the goddess of the mountain Fuji-yama (see also 'Pilgrimages', page 79). Each village – and often each person – has its own shrine, which contains an object sacred to the god. In a village shrine there are rooms for worship and ceremonial dancing. Priests recite prayers daily and make offerings of green twigs.

Each shrine holds an annual festival some time between June and October, which often takes the form of thanksgiving for harvest. The whole community turns out for these colourful, joyful occasions. They last for two or three days, during which the shrine grounds are filled with a variety of stalls selling things such as sweets, toys and goldfish.

5 On the first Thanksgiving Day

*Traditional North American
Arranged by Theron Haithwaite*

Reverently

On the first Thanks-giv-ing Day, Pil-grims went to church to pray,
Thanked the Lord for sun and rain, Thanked Him for the fields of grain.
Now Thanks-giv-ing comes a-gain: Praise the Lord as they did then.
Thank Him for the sun and rain, Thank Him for the fields of grain.

Recorders

Thanksgiving

Thanksgiving is celebrated on the fourth Thursday in November in the United States and on the second Monday of October in Canada. It started with the Pilgrim Fathers who probably based it on the English harvest festival. When they settled in America in 1619, conditions were very bad and the governor was so relieved when the harvest was safely gathered that he ordered a three-day feast. The local Indians were invited as well and added turkey and venison to the ducks, geese and fish of the settlers. The meal was eaten on huge tables out of doors.

Now Thanksgiving is a family occasion with traditional dishes such as turkey and pumpkin pie. Abraham Lincoln decreed that it should be 'a day of thanksgiving and praise to our beneficent Father' and so now it is also a time for church services and giving thanks for blessings of all kinds.

6 Cheshire souling song

Traditional English

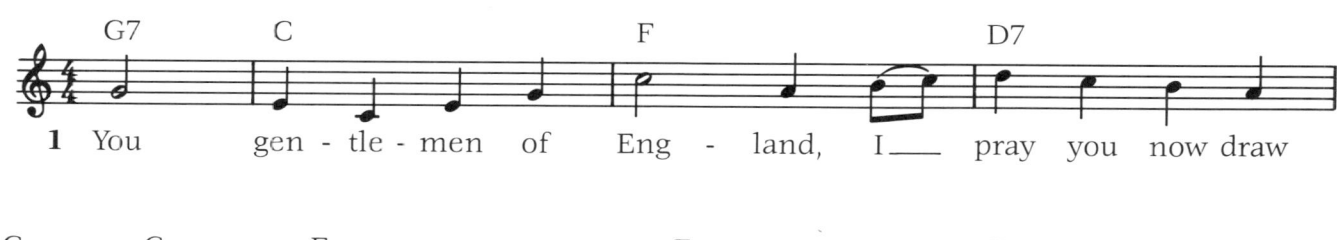

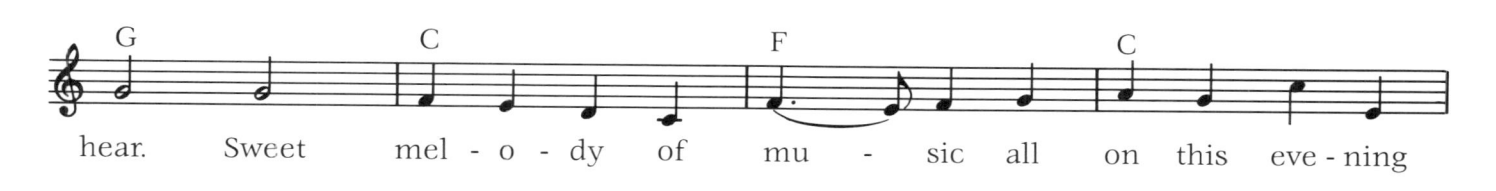

1. You gentlemen of England, I pray you now draw near,
And then these few short lines you very soon shall hear.
Sweet melody of music all on this evening clear,
For we are come a-souling for apples and strong beer.

2. Step down into your cellar, and see what you can find,
If your barrels are not empty, we hope you will prove kind;
We hope you will prove kind with your apples and strong beer,
We'll come no more a-souling until another year.

3. Cold winter it is coming on, dark, dirty, wet and cold;
To try your good nature, this night we do make bold;
This night we do make bold with your apples and strong beer,
We'll come no more a-souling until another year.

Festivals and Seasons

4 All the houses that we've been at, we've had both meat and drink,
So now we're dry with travelling, we hope you'll on us think;
We hope you'll on us think with your apples and strong beer,
For we'll come no more a-souling until another year.

5 God bless the master of this house, and the mistress also,
And all the little children that round the table go;
Likewise your men and maidens, your cattle and your store,
And all that lies within your gates we wish you ten times more;

Repeat last two lines of music { We wish you ten times more with your apples and strong beer.
And we'll come no more a-souling until another year.

All Saints' Day

The first of November is All Saints' Day, once known as 'All Martyrs'. On this day all the saints, who are too numerous for each to be named, are commemorated. At one time, parties of men and children used to go round 'souling'. This meant calling at the houses of all the people in the neighbourhood who were fairly well off, to ask for gifts of cakes, ale, apples, money, or even simply left-over food. Some of these cakes were specially baked. In order to help to persuade the householders to give, the soulers would perform a short play or perhaps sing a song.

A recipe for soul cakes

1400 g flour
100 g butter (or 250 g if the cakes are to be extra rich)
250 g sugar
2 teaspoons yeast
2 eggs
Allspice to taste, and sufficient milk to make it into a light paste.

Put the mixture (without the sugar or spice) to rise before the fire for half an hour, then add the sugar, and enough allspice to flavour it well. Make into rather flat buns, and bake.
(Shropshire recipe)

7 A happy time

Mary Plummer

Happily

1. A happy time is Diwali, When we light the twinkling lights. A happy time is Diwali, Happy days and nights.

2. A happy time is Diwali,
   Fireworks blaze and candles glow.
   A happy time is Diwali,
   The lights our happiness show.

Pitched Percussion or Descant Recorders

Use the underneath part of the right hand of the piano as a simple alto part.

20 Festivals and Seasons

Diwali

The most important Hindu festival, Diwali, is celebrated in October/November each year and lasts four or five days. Its name is a shortened form of *Deepawalee* – a line of lamps – and it is a festival of lights, when Lakshmi, the goddess of wealth, is particularly remembered.

The festival may be celebrated in different ways in different parts of the world, but all the stories relate the triumph of good over evil.

This is what happens in some parts of India: On the first day a lamp is lit to Yama, god of death, and Hindus remember the victory of Lord Krishna over the demon Narakaasura. Narakaasura kidnapped girls and women and invoked Vishnu to help destroy Krishna. Vishnu appealed to Krishna who granted the demon one wish in recognition of the few good deeds he had done. Narakaasura wished that that day should become a day of feasting. So on the first day of Diwali new clothes are worn, and there is feasting and firecrackers.

On the second day Lakshmi is worshipped, her wealth symbolised by a gold ornament or rupee. Accounts for the year are closed and the financial year ends. Doors and windows are left open to welcome Lakshmi, rangoli (attractive patterns) are drawn on the floor near the entrance of the house, and the house and its surroundings are illuminated so that she can see her way.

On the fourth day presents are exchanged. The fifth day is Sister's Day. A man visits his sister's house where he has a ceremonial bath, after which she puts kumkum (a dot of red powder) on his forehead and waves a lamp in circular motion before him to ward off evil. This custom is based on the legend that on this day Yama, god of death, dined with his sister Yamuna.

In some parts of northern India the legend of Rama and Sita (told in the epic poem *The Ramayana*) is particularly remembered. While Rama was away, Ravana, the demon king of Sri Lanka, carried away his wife Sita. After many adventures Rama (who is considered to be an incarnation of the god Vishnu) was able to conquer Ravana with the help of the goddess Durga and returned home to great rejoicing. In some towns fireworks commemorate the burning of Ravana's capital. Girls visit neighbouring houses carrying a lamp in a large clay pot with many holes in it, representing the head of a foreign tyrant who was pierced by arrows and later beheaded. Diwali is a time of new beginnings.

The Sikhs also celebrate the festival, but for different reasons. It was at Diwali that the sixth Guru was released from prison and met by Sikhs carrying candles. They also celebrate the founding of the Golden Temple at Amritsar, which is lavishly illuminated with candles at this time.

8 Oh Chanukah

Traditional Jewish

With vigour

Oh Chanukah, Oh Chanukah, come light the menorah, Let's have a party, we'll all dance the horah. Gather round the table, we'll give you a treat: Dreidels to play with and latkes to eat. And while we are playing, The candles are burning low. One for each night, they will shed a sweet light to re-

22 Festivals and Seasons

mind us of days long a-go. mind us of days long a-go.

Yemei ha Chanukah

Chanukat mikdashenu

Begil uvesimchah memalim et libenu

Layla vayom s'viyonenu yesov

Sufganiyot nochal bam larov
Ha-inu hadliku
Nerot chanukah rabim
Al hanisim ve-al hanifla-ot
Asher cholelu hamaccabim.

(Hebrew by A. Evranin)

Oy Chanukah,
Oy Chanukah a yom tov a sheynem

A lustiger a frelacher
Nito noch a zoyner

Alle nacht in dreidlach shpiln mir

Zudig heyse latkes essen on a shir.
Geshvinder tzindt kinder
Di dininke lichtelach ohn
Zogt 'Al hanisim', loibt Gott far di nisim
Unkumt gicher tantzen in kohn.

(Yiddish by M. Riversman)

Pitched percussion

Could invent interesting rhythms on the note D, for example:

A hand drum could also play this rhythm.

Chanukah

Chanukah is the Jewish festival of light, falling in November/December. It celebrates the victory of Judah the Maccabee over the Syrians, who had forbidden the Jews to worship their God and had put idols in their temple. The first thing the Jews did was to restore the temple; some say this took eight days. After a long search they had enough oil to light the temple lamp for one day, but by some miracle it burned for eight. Both of these are possible reasons for the festival now lasting eight days. In homes and synagogues an eight-branched candlestick is lit, one candle for each day of the festival. There is an additional branch, making nine, for holding the servant candle to light the others. Special prayers are said and while the candles burn no work should be done.

Presents are given, special games are played and food is eaten. One game involves a *dreidel* or spinning top with four sides, each marked with the Hebrew letters N, G, H, Sh – for *Nes Gadol Hayah Sham* (a great miracle happened there). Legend has it that this was one of the games played by the Jews to trick the Syrians when they were in the middle of their prayers. Potato pancakes (*latkes*) and doughnuts (*sufganiyot*) are the traditional foods eaten at Chanukah. Both of these are fried in oil to remind Jews of the miracle of the oil.

9 Munji Aziz ka jnumdin
Jesus's birth

Urdu carol collected from Ella Samuel

Lively
Verse

1 Aaj mun-ji a-ziz kaa j-num-din hoo-aa. Sub lo-go ke vaas-te mu-jas-sum hoo-aa, Sub lo-go ke vaas-te mu-jas-sum hoo-aa, Sub lo-go ke vaas-te, sub lo-go ke vaas-te mu-jas-sum hoo-aa.

Come let's ce-le-brate Je-sus' birth-day to-day. And how He is born here for ev'-ry-one's sake, And how He is born here for ev'-ry-one's sake, And how He is born here, And how He is born here for ev'-ry-one's sake.

Chorus

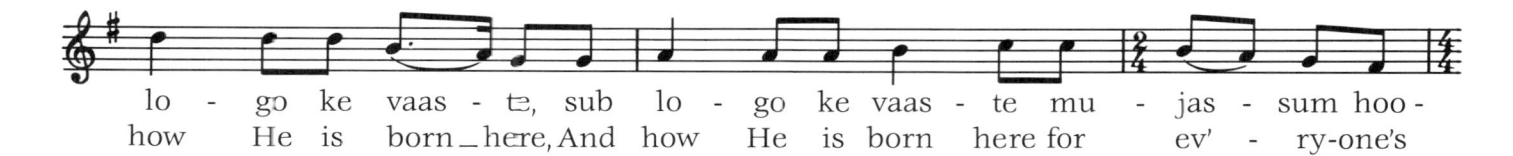

Aa-s-ma-ni ho-wa chal-ti shi-faf ki na-di be-he-ti Pa-ki-z gee vah de-ti, Hal-le-lu-ya sa-na-ho.

There's a cool re-fresh-ing breeze and a ri-ver of pure wa-ter flow-ing, Pu-ri-fy-ing all things, Hal-le-lu-jah, praise the Lord.

2 Gadario ne deka oojahla ooska

Bheren chh-or munji ko sijda kiya (*twice*)

Bheren chh-or munji, bheren chh-or munji ko sijda kiya.
Chorus

Festivals and Seasons

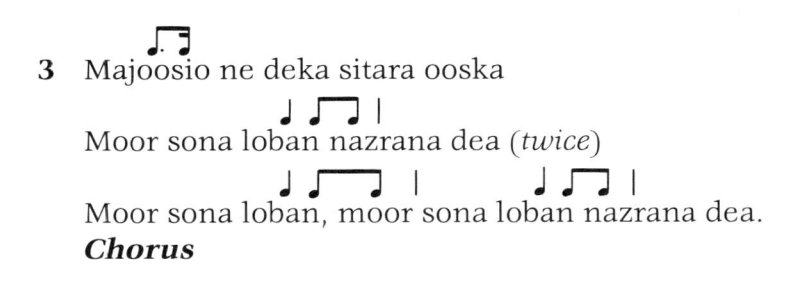

3 Majoosio ne deka sitara ooska
   Moor sona loban nazrana dea (*twice*)
   Moor sona loban, moor sona loban nazrana dea.
   Chorus

4 Sab logo ne deka oojahla ooska
   Sab kaam chh-or munji ko sijda kiya (*twice*)
   Sab kaam chh-or munji, sab kaam chh-or munji ko sijda kiya.
   Chorus

*Some consonants are sounded as separate syllables, for example, 'chhor' = choru ('u' as in **put**), 'loban' = lobanu.*

2 When those humble shepherds first saw that great light,
   They left all their flocks for to worship the Lord, (*twice*)
   They left all their flocks, they left all their flocks for to worship the Lord.
   Chorus

3 The wise men set out when they saw that bright star;
   They offered him gifts, gold and incense and myrrh, (*twice*)
   They offered him gifts, they offered him gifts, gold and incense and myrrh.
   Chorus

4 So ev'ryone came to see Jesus' bright light;
   They left all their work for to worship the Lord, (*twice*)
   They left all their work, they left all their work for to worship the Lord.
   Chorus

Christmas

This is the Christian festival when the birth of Jesus, whom Christians believe to be the Son of God, is celebrated. Stories are told of his birth in a stable to the Virgin Mary, the worshipping of the shepherds and the pilgrimage of the three kings or wise men. Presents are exchanged and special foods, such as mince pies and turkey, are eaten in the West.

There are many customs associated with Christmas all over the world. Some of them – such as the decorating of the house with evergreens, mistletoe and the yule log – have been incorporated into the Christmas celebration, but are of pagan origin.

10 Charni may bahar
Joy in the manager

Urdu carol collected from Ella Samuel

Happily
Chorus

Cha - r - ni may lu - g ee hai ba - har A - j Yes - su pai - da hoo - e.
Look how He is ly - ing in a man - ger, See Je - sus born on this day.

Fine

Khu - shi - a - n ma - na - i sun - sa - r
Let the whole world sing out with re - joic - ing,

A - j Yes - su pai - da hoo - e.
See Je - sus born on this day.

Verse

1 Be - th - le -
In Beth - le -

he - m may gu - l - shun khi - la hei, gu - l - shun khi - la hei.
hem there is a new flo - wer in bloom now, a new flo - wer in bloom now.

Ar - she ba - ree say see - taa ra gi - raa - hai, see -
See a new star has come down from se - venth hea - ven, come

taa - ra gi - raa - hai. Ma - joo - si - yun kaa de - ka hai pi -
down from se - venth hea - ven. Look how the kings a - dore the ti - ny

ya - r A - j Yes - su pai - da hoo - e.
ba - by, See Je - sus born on this day.

26 Festivals and Seasons

*The line marked * is omitted in the other verses, the singer moving straight from the end of the chorus (**Fine**) to the next verse.*

Chorus

2   Charni may deka he majoosio ne ake, majoosio ne ake. (*twice*)
    Sejda kiya he Nazre charhake, Nazre charhake,
    Jhuk jhuk jai bar bar,
    Aj Yessu paida hooe.

Chorus

3   Har ghar khushiun say bhar bhar aye, bhar bhar aye. (*twice*)
    Har dill Yessu ji ka mangal gai, ka mangal gai,
    Tum caro khushiun hazar.
    Aj Yessu paida hooe.

Chorus

*Some consonants are sounded as separate syllables: 'charni' = char**u**ni ('u' as in **put**), 'aj' = arj**u**.*

Chorus

2   Three kings now see the babe lying in a manger, lying in a manger. (*twice*)
    Then they give Him their lovely presents, their lovely presents.
    They bow down many times before the baby.
    See Jesus born on this day.

Chorus

3   See how they're filled with joy and their hearts are rejoicing, and their hearts are rejoicing. (*twice*)
    Jesus's birth has made everyone rejoice now, everyone rejoice now.
    Let us all join together in rejoicing.
    See Jesus born on this day.

Chorus

Epiphany

Twelve days after Christmas, on 6 January, Christians celebrate the festival of the Epiphany. (Epiphany is from a Greek word meaning 'manifestation'.) It is then that they remember the arrival of the three kings or wise men (magi) at the stable in Bethlehem. This is the first account of people who were not Jews visiting Jesus. Their gifts, as described in St Matthew's gospel, were symbolic. Gold showed that Jesus was a king, and frankincense is associated with worship. Myrrh, which is a spice used in the burial of the dead, showed that he would suffer.

Festivals and Seasons

11 Master Hee-haw

Words translated from traditional Latin by Arthur Scholey
Music traditional, arranged by June Tillman

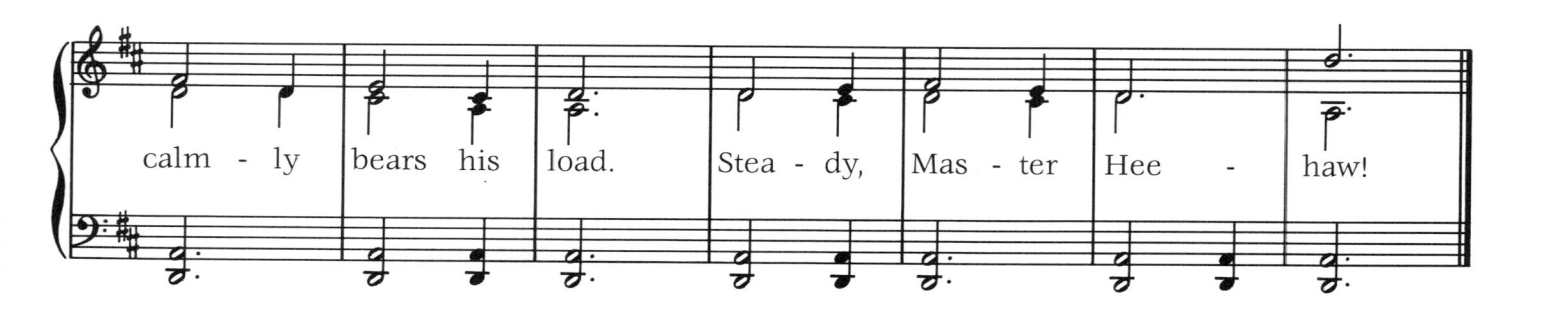

Slow

1 From the East and long ago, Came the Donkey, sure and slow, Even when we use the goad, Still he calmly bears his load. Steady, Master Hee-haw!

Festivals and Seasons

Slow 2 Born he was upon the heath,
　　　　　Long his ears and strong his teeth,
　　　　　Chomping thistle, barley, corn,
　　　　　See the path his jaws have worn.
　　　　　　　Hungry Master Hee-haw!

Faster 3 Now he leaps as in a race!
　　　　　　Gone the dromedary's pace,
　　　　　　Look, he's passing hare and roe –
　　　　　　What a wonder! See him go!
　　　　　　　　Speedy Master Hee-haw!

Fast! 4 Jordan's crossed and now he climbs –
　　　　　Quite forgotten olden times?
　　　　　Yes, he has no thought for them,
　　　　　Galloping into Bethlehem.
　　　　　　Welcome Master Hee-haw!

Alternative words

1　Orientis partibus
　Adventavit asinus,
　Pulcher et fortissimus,
　Sarcinis aptissimus.
　Hez, sire Ane, hez.

2　Aurum de Arabia
　Thus et myrrham de Saba,
　Tulit in ecclesia
　Virtus asinaria.
　Hez, sire Ane, hez.

3　Amen, dicas, asine;
　Iam satur de gramine;
　Amen, amen itera,
　Aspernare vetera.
　Hez, sire Ane, hez.

Pitched Percussion　　**Tambour**

Recorders

Verse 1　*Unaccompanied melody (slow)*
Verse 2　*Melody and drone on pitched percussion and tambour (slow)*
Verse 3　*Melody, alto part and drone on recorders (faster)*
Verse 4　*Melody, alto part and drone (faster)*

The festival of the donkey

This Latin carol was originally sung by pilgrims en route to Compostela in Spain. Later it was sung on 14 January in France each year at the Festival of the Donkey, and it is the French carol which forms the basis of this version.

The Festival of the Donkey commemorated the Flight into Egypt and involved a procession through the streets with a girl representing Mary on a donkey. The donkey was led into the church where a very merry service was held.

12 Matsukazari

Japanese New Year's song

Traditional Japanese
Translated by Rosemary Jacques

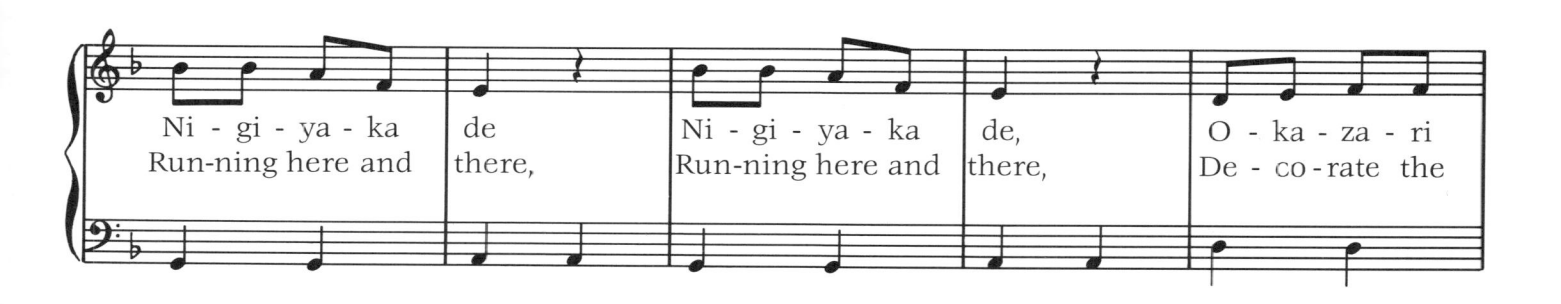

Lively

1. Hi - to - tsu to ya,_____ Hi - to - yo a - ku - re - ba,
   On the eve of New Year's, Bu - sy peo - ple, hap - py peo - ple,
   Ni - gi - ya - ka de, Ni - gi - ya - ka de, O - ka - za - ri
   Run-ning here and there, Run-ning here and there, De - co - rate the
   ta - te - ta - ru ma - tsu - ka - za - ri,_____ Ma - tsu - ka - za - ri.
   bam-boo trees to ce - le-brate the day,_____ ce - le-brate the day.

2. On the eve of New Year's,

   Paper streamers, fresh plum blossoms
   Hang above the door,
   Hang above the door,

   Telling all who pass by to have a happy day,
   Have a happy day.

Festivals and Seasons

3 On the day of New Year's,
Games are played and songs are sung to
Celebrate the day,
Celebrate the day.
People come to wish each other happy New Year's Day,
Happy New Year's Day.

Use the left hand of the piano part as a pitched percussion part.

Descant Recorders

Japanese New Year

In Japan, *Ganjitsu*, or New Year, is the most important holiday, and equivalent to Christmas in the West. It lasts for three days and is celebrated with family reunions, homecomings, special foods and decorations, many of which have special meanings such as good health, long life, sincerity, cleanliness, and so on. An important part of this festival is the first visit of the year to a Shinto shrine. A piece of soil containing the family god, *Uji-gami*, is sometimes sent to those members of the family unable to get home for the festival.

13 Chinese New Year

Collected from Wen-Ying Hsiung-Chen

Brightly

Hap-py New Year to you! Hap-py New Year to you! The New Year it comes round year by year. The sound of the fire-crack-ers brings to my mind the mem'-ries of by-gone days. Hap-py New Year to you! Hap-py New Year to you! The New Year it comes round year by year. Sea-sons change. Time flies past like an ar-row in the sky, Past

32 Festivals and Seasons

hap'-nings are blown a-way like smoke. We have suf-fered pains and sor-rows e-nough. May the New Year bring us all good luck. Hap-py New Year to you! Hap-py New Year to you! The New Year it comes round year by year. The New Year it comes round year by year.

Festivals and Seasons 33

Chinese New Year

This is the main Chinese festival and falls between mid January and mid February. It lasts 15 days, although usually less in Chinese communities overseas, during which time streets are decorated with lanterns, banners and flags for the colourful processions with music and dancing, like the Lion Dance. Dragons are popular, especially in the Year of the Dragon which falls every ten years – 1976, 1986, and so on.

In the home the preparations begin a week earlier with special cleaning, for tradition says that a report on the home is made by a kitchen god to the emperor of Heaven before the festival begins. The firecrackers and incense on New Year's Eve welcome back these gods. It is a time of family reunions and new beginnings when old quarrels are forgotten. Houses are decorated with flowers, fruits and lanterns, children are given 'lucky money' in red envelopes, and coins are shaken from the 'money tree' to bring good fortune. Red for luck and gold for prosperity are prominent. Business accounts should be settled and all debts paid before the New Year. Ancestors are honoured. Red scrolls bearing messages of happiness, prosperity and long life are pasted on the walls. Knives and scissors are put away so that no one will cut the continuity of luck for the year to come.

Special foods such as *jiaozi* are prepared. *Jiaozi* are white flour dumplings, some of which contain hidden coins. Other foods have exotic names linked to the celebrations – eggs are 'silver ingots', mushrooms are 'opportunities' and chicken is 'Phoenix' (new life). The greeting *Kungshi fa ts'ai* – 'a happy and prosperous New Year' – is exchanged.

14 Chinese lantern song

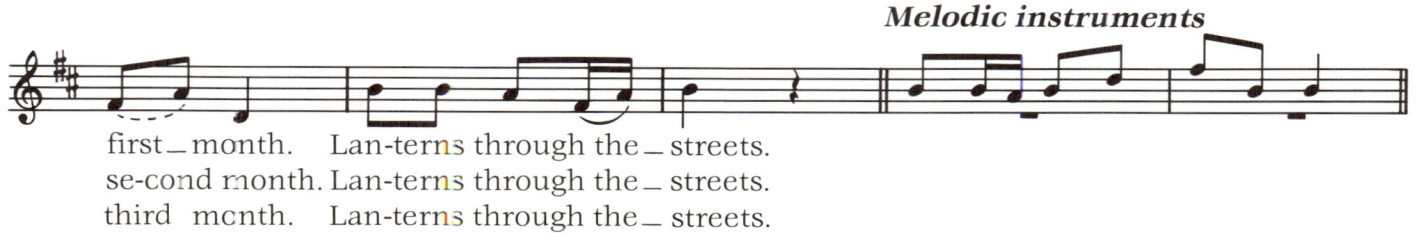

Translated by Stephen Jones

At a moderate speed
Melodic instruments

Let's go and see the lan-terns to-day,   lan - terns in the

Melodic instruments

first month.   Lan-terns through the streets.
se-cond month. Lan-terns through the streets.
third month.   Lan-terns through the streets.

Festivals and Seasons

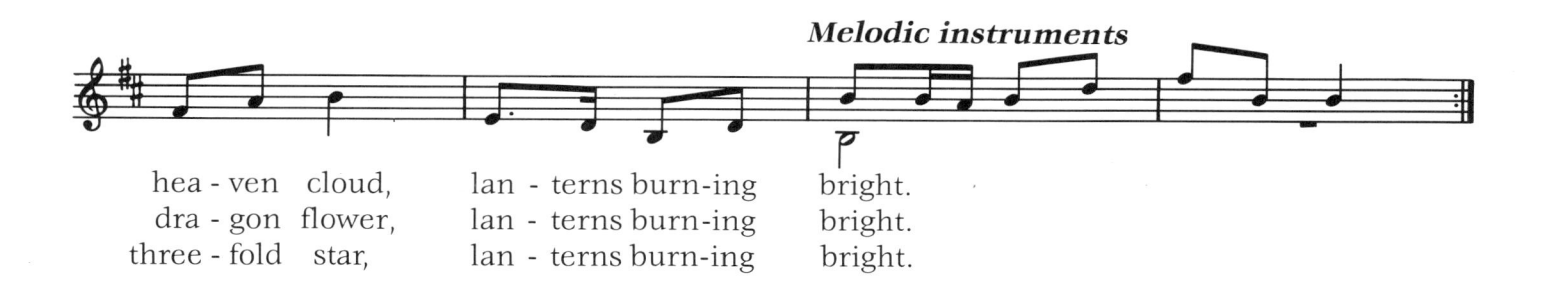

Melodic instruments

What are the lan-terns we can see? We can see the

Melodic instruments

hea - ven cloud, lan - terns burn-ing bright.
dra - gon flower, lan - terns burn-ing bright.
three - fold star, lan - terns burn-ing bright.

Add finger cymbals on the first beat of each bar.

Pitched Percussion

Chinese lantern festival

This song, which comes from central China, describes three of the many festivals in the Chinese calendar, although changes in government have meant that they are not celebrated as they once were. The one in the first month is probably the Lantern festival, *Teng Chieh*, which comes at the end of the New Year celebrations on the fifteenth day. Brightly-coloured lanterns made from silk, glass, paper, straw and imitation pearls represent the coming of light and warmth after the darkness of winter. The Chinese New Year is in February/March.

The festival in the second month is probably *Ch'ing Ming*, the Festival of Pure Brightness, one month after the Lantern festival and a time when families get together, visit family graves and offer gifts to their ancestors.

15 My name is Purim

Traditional Jewish

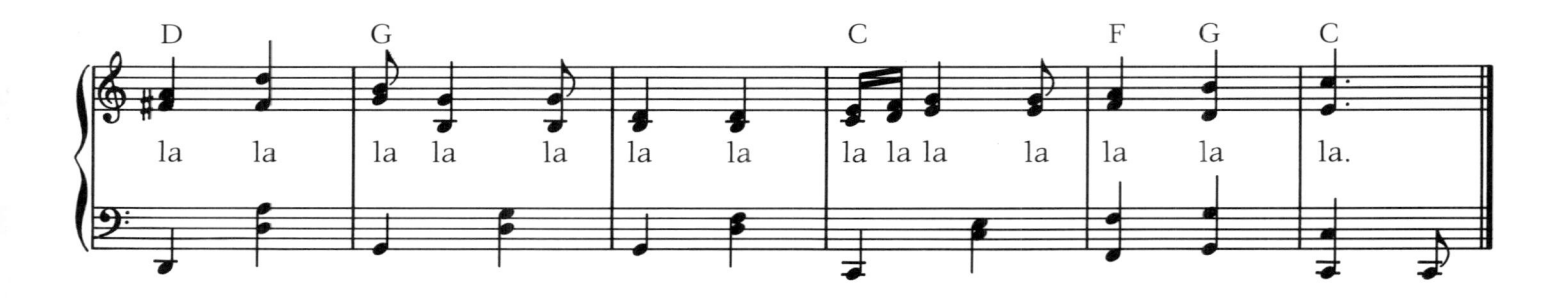

At a moderate pace

1 My name is Purim and I come, Great fun and frolic bringing. Just once a year I visit you To cheer you with my singing.

Chorus
La la la la la la la la la la la la la la la la la la la.

2 Hurrah Purim! Hurrah Purim!
I love your merry drumming
And if I had my way, Purim,
Each month you would be coming.
Chorus

3 Oh, Mr Purim tell us why
We see you only yearly?
Please make it once or twice a week
Because we love you dearly.
Chorus

Festivals and Seasons

Recorders

Pitched Percussion

You could substitute any festival for Purim in the song, for example:

Christmas (see 'Charni may bahar', page 26)
Eid (see 'Aye re aye', page 60)
Holi (see 'Holi with Shyam', page 50)
Wesak (see 'Buddha Lord we offer', page 58)

Purim

This joyful Jewish festival is celebrated in February/March. It recalls the story of Esther, who saved the Jewish people by pleading with the king who was going to destroy all Jews. The king was under the influence of an official named Haman who arranged for lots – *purim* – to be cast to decide how this was to be done. Haman intended to start with Esther's uncle, Mordecai, but thanks to Esther, Haman was hanged on his own gallows.

The day before Purim is a fast to remind the Jews how Esther fasted for three days while praying to God for courage to help her save her people. In the service in the synagogue on the festival day, children are encouraged to make as much noise as possible, some with homemade instruments called graggers (rattles), whenever the name of Haman is mentioned. There is a festive dinner with candles, prayers, party games and special foods such as *hamantaschen*, three-cornered pastries filled with poppy seeds to remind people of Haman's three-cornered hat.

Purim is a time, especially in Israel, of plays, masquerades, parades, carnivals and dressing up. Presents are given and gifts sent to the poor. It is a time also when some people remember more recent escapes from danger.

16 Cân y grempog
The pancake song

Traditional Welsh
Translated by O. Griffiths and Roy Palmer

Wraig y tŷ a'r teulu da, Os gwelwch chi'n dda, ga'i grempog? Mae
Mam rhy dlawd i byrnu blawd A 'Nhad rhyddiog i weithio. Os
gwelwch chi'n dda ga'i grempog? Mae 'ngheg i'n grimp am grempog. Os nad oes menyn
yn y tŷ Rhowch lwyad fawr o driog. Ac os nad oes triog
yn y tŷ Rhowch grempog fawr gynddeiriog, Gynddeiriog, gynddeiriog.

Lady of this big, fine house, Please give me a pancake.
Mam's too poor to buy any flour, And Dad's too lazy to work, so,
Please give me a pancake, I'm dying for a pancake. If you've no butter
in the house, Give a spoonful of treacle, And if you've no treacle
in the house, Give me a great, big pancake, A pancake, a pancake.

This chant is best sung unaccompanied.

Pancake day

Shrove Tuesday falls in February or March (depending on the date of Easter) and is the day before the beginning of Lent on Ash Wednesday. On this day people traditionally went to the church to confess their sins and be forgiven. (The word *shriven*, or *shrove*, means 'forgiven'.) As Lent was once kept as a period of fasting and solemnity, Shrove Tuesday was a time for merrymaking and using up all the leftover stocks of fat, butter and eggs which were forbidden during Lent; hence the origin of the pancake. Religions other than Christianity also have periods of fasting, though for different reasons.

17 Great is His love

Joseph Gelineau

With dignity

Solo: 1 O give thanks to the Lord for He is good.

Chorus: Great is His love, love without end!

Solo: Give thanks to the God of gods,

Chorus: Great is His love, love without end!

Solo: Give thanks to the Lord of lords,

Chorus: Great is His love, love without end!

2 Who a-lone has wrought mar-vel-lous works,
(Great. . .)

Whose wis-dom it was made the skies,
(Great. . .)

Who fixed the earth firm-ly on the seas,
(Great. . .)

3 It was He who made the great lights,
(Great. . .)

The sun to rule in the day,
(Great. . .)

The moon and stars in the night,
(Great. . .)

4 The first-born of the Egyptians He smote,
(Great. . .)

Brought Israel out from their midst,
(Great. . .)

Arm outstretched, with power in His hand,
(Great. . .)

5 He divided the Red Sea in two,
(Great. . .)

Give thanks to the God of gods,
(Great. . .)

Give thanks to the Lord of lords,
(Great. . .)

6 Through the desert His people He led,
(Great. . .)

Nations in their greatness He struck
(Great. . .)

Kings in their splendour He slew,
(Great. . .)

7 He let Israel inherit their land,
(Great. . .)

On his servants their land He bestowed,
(Great. . .)

He remembered us in our distress,
(Great. . .)

8 And He snatched us away from our foes,
(Great. . .)

He gives food to all living things,
(Great. . .)

To the God of heaven give thanks,
(Great. . .)

40   Festivals and Seasons

Gelineau's version of Psalm 136 consists of a free setting of the verse followed by a choral section. The verse is recited by a soloist to the long notes in the accompaniment, so that the first verse may come out like this:

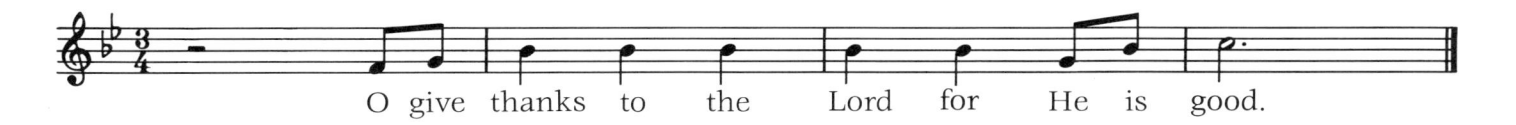

O give thanks to the Lord for He is good.

The later verses have the bar lines indicated.

Pesach (Passover)

This is an eight-day Jewish festival celebrated in the spring when the deliverance of the children of Israel from slavery in Egypt is especially remembered. The story of the Exodus is told to the children and there is a special meal called the Seder, where songs are sung and prayers of thanksgiving said.

Before the Seder the house is thoroughly cleaned and any traces of yeast burned. The bread for the meal is *matza*, unleavened bread, like that eaten in haste by the Jews when they fled from Egypt. There are also bitter herbs, *maror*, to remind Jews of the cruelty of the Pharaoh and these are dipped in a mixture of chopped apples and nuts, *charoset*, which looks like the clay used by the Jews to make the bricks for building Pharaoh's cities. Parsley is dipped in salt water; green parsley celebrates new life and the salt water recalls the tears shed by the Jews in their slavery. An egg on the Seder plate reminds them of new life in spring and the lamb bone recalls the roasted lamb that the Jews ate on the first Passover night.

People may eat their meal sitting on pillows as a reminder that they were once slaves but now are free. There is an extra cup of wine on the table called the Cup of Elijah; the story goes that Elijah, the prophet, visits homes at Seder to bring peace and freedom.

The song speaks of this occasion and also looks forward to the coming of the Messiah which was foretold by Elijah.

Festivals and Seasons

18 Whey he day?

Anthony Pierre

With vigour

Chorus

Whey he day? Whey he day? Whey he day, mi Lard? Whey he day? Whey he day? Whey he day, mi Lard? Whey he day? Whey he day? Whey he day, mi Lard? Ah cyant fine He, fine He at all.

Fine **To Coda last time**

Verse

1. Ah want to see de man from Ga-la-lee, Ah want to see de man who

42   Festivals and Seasons

set me free, Ah want to see de man who die for me, Ah cyant fine He, fine He at all.

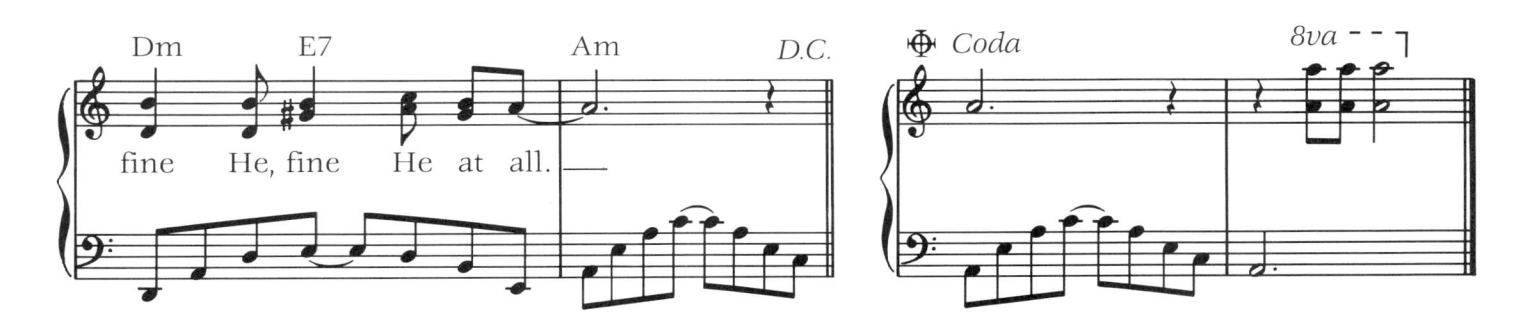

2 Ah want to see de man who bleed for me.
   Ah want to see de man dey scourge for me.
   Ah want to see dis man from Galalee,
   Ah cyant fine He, fine He at all.
   Chorus

This song is from the Caribbean. 'Whey he day' means 'Where is he?'

3 Whey de man who make de bline to see?
   Whey de man who set de captive free?
   Whey de man who make de lame to walk?
   An de lil dumb boy to talk?
   Chorus

The life of Jesus

Christians believe that Jesus, who was brought up in the home of a Jewish carpenter, is the Son of God. There are few accounts of his early life, but at about the age of 30 he began travelling with a group of friends, spending much of this time around Galilee where he performed many miracles of healing, as set out in verse 3 of this song. He made the religious leaders angry. Eventually he was taken to the Roman authorities, who had him scourged and crucified.

Festivals and Seasons

19 Arnaki ke likos
The lamb and the wolf

Greek folk song collected from Maria Roussou, translated by Nitsa Sergides
English lyrics and accompaniment by Jean Gilbert

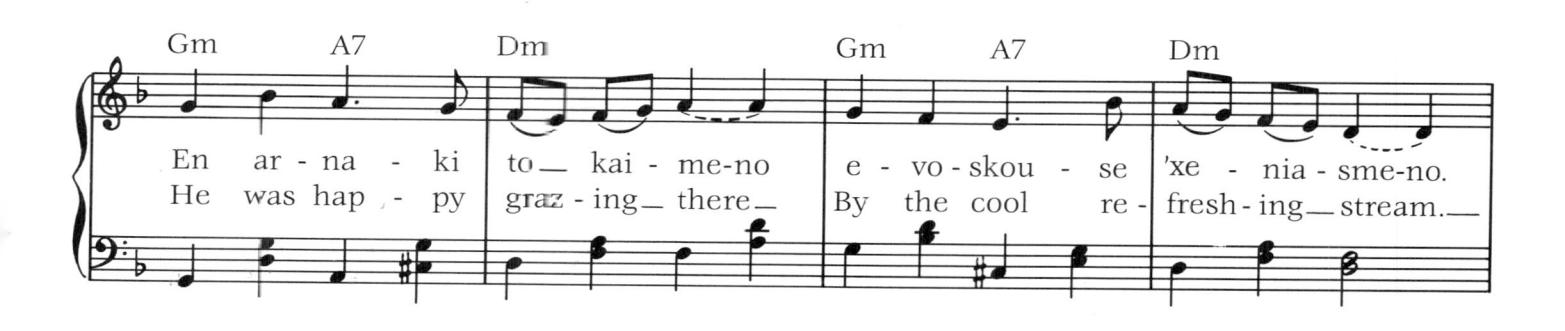

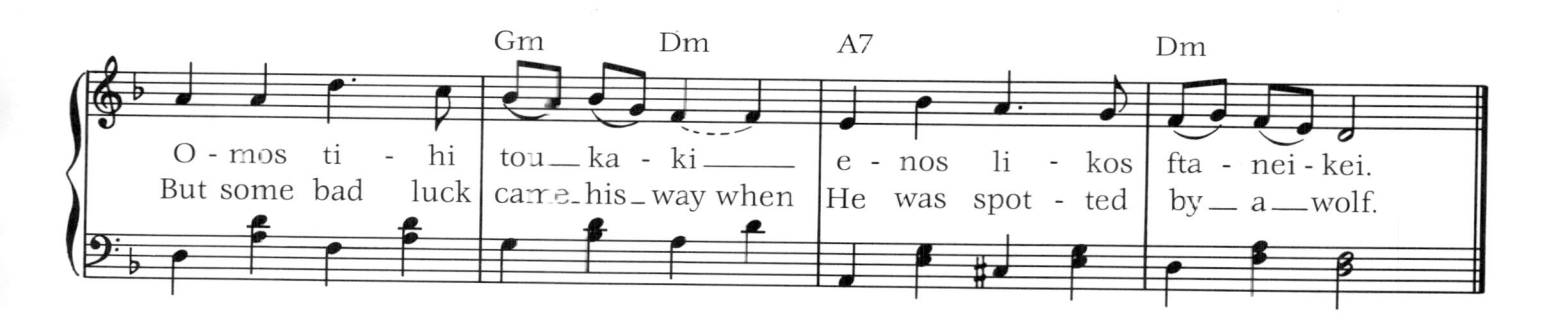

1. Mia fo - ra kie - na ke - ro se li - va - di dro - se - ro.
   En ar - na - ki to kai - me - no e - vo - skou - se 'xe - nia - sme - no.
   O - mos ti - hi tou ka - ki e - nos li - kos fta - nei - kei.

   Once there was a lit - tle lamb Graz - ing near a lit - tle stream.
   He was hap - py graz - ing there By the cool re - fresh - ing stream.
   But some bad luck came his way when He was spot - ted by a wolf.

44 Festivals and Seasons

2 'S'epiasa tou ipe eftis
Klefti tha timorithis
Irtes is ton potamo mou
Ke mou pinis to neró mou'
'Ohi, ipe to arnaki
Evlepa to livadaki.'

3 'Omos persi ena vradi
M'evrises mes to skotadi'
'Persi, ipe to kaimeno
Ma den imoun gennimeno'
'Kala legis ego sfallo
T'adelpaki sou to allo.'

4 'Adelpákin sou omóno
Pos den eho ime mono'
'Tis psefties na tis afiseis
Treha na dikigorisis'
Ke to stoma tou anigi
Ke to distiho to pnigei.

Add a strong drumbeat in the chorus.

2 'I have caught you, I have seen
You've been drinking from my stream.
You must die for stealing my water
You're the thief who comes to my stream.'
'No, I was not drinking water,
I was grazing by the stream.'

3 'You were rude about my shadow
Cursing it one day last year.'
'No, oh no, that was not me
I was not even born last year.'
'Well said, then it was your brother,
I mistook you,' said the wolf.

4 'Please believe me, I'm the only one,
I don't have a brother at home.'
'That's a lie, you can't fool me,
You will need a lawyer to win.'
Then he opened wide his mouth
And soon the little lamb was gone.

Easter Sunday

Easter is the major Christian festival. Christians believe that Jesus is the Son of God and that, after being crucified on the hill of Calvary just outside Jerusalem, he rose from the dead. His body had been laid in a rocky tomb and on Easter Sunday morning some of his disciples came looking for him. Mary Magdalen met the risen Jesus in the garden. When Simon Peter came to the tomb and found Jesus's body gone, two angels told him that Jesus was risen.

Festivals and Seasons

20 H'ristos anesti
Jesus has risen

Greek Easter hymn, translated by Nitsa Sergides

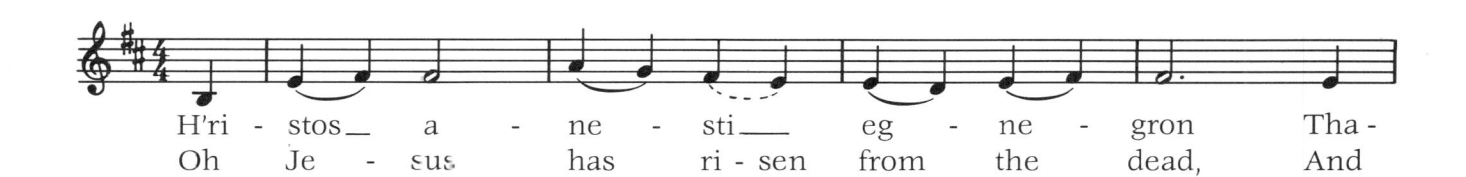

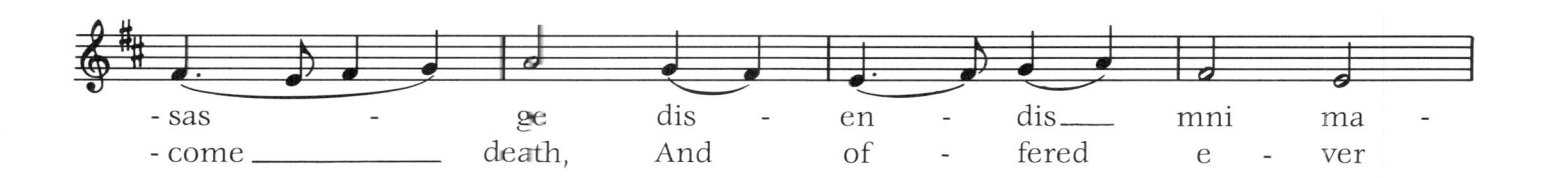

H'ri - stos_ a - ne - sti_ eg - ne - gron Tha - na - do tha - na - don ba di - - - sas - ge dis - en - dis_ mni ma - si zo - in ha - ri sa - me_ nos.

Oh Je - sus has ri - sen from the dead, And He_ has o - ver - come death, He has o - ver - come_ death, And of - fered ever - last - ing_ life, e - ver - last - ing_ life.

This Easter hymn is sung in all churches in Cyprus on Easter Sunday. Sing it unaccompanied, very clearly and not too fast.

46 Festivals and Seasons

Easter in Cyprus

On Palm Sunday, people take olive branches to church and wave them as they walk in procession behind the priest as a symbol of the welcome given to Christ as he entered Jerusalem. The olive branches are left in the church for 40 days and then are taken home. They are lit, put into a special pot to smoulder, and carried around the house so that hatred will be banished.

During Holy Week, icons in churches are covered with black cloths and villagers attend services every evening. On Holy Thursday, single girls drink vinegar in memory of Christ's suffering on the cross, and prepare garlands to hang by the cross.

On Good Friday boys and girls dress in white and sing songs about the injustice of the death of Jesus. An *epitaph*, which is a carved structure decorated with rosemary and flowers containing an icon of Jesus, is carried through the streets in the evening and is guarded overnight by the older women.

On Saturday people bake cakes, prepare plaited bread topped with sesame seeds, and dye eggs. The lamb is prepared for the main meal on Easter Sunday, when it will be barbecued and eaten with stuffed vine leaves, roast potatoes or macaroni moussaka, followed by fresh oranges and homemade cakes.

The Easter Sunday service begins with the priest bringing out three lighted candles, from which the villagers light their own candles to take home. The black cloths are lifted from the icons and the words 'God is risen' are sung. In the afternoon an effigy of Judas is burnt on a bonfire and there is a firework display. People eat cakes and play games with hardboiled eggs and there is another church service before the lamb is eaten at the main meal of the day.

21 The Son of God

Cynthia Allen

1. The Son of God gave His life for us. He died on the cross on Calvary. There was no one with Him in His misery, There was no one with Him in His misery.

Chorus
The Son of God is risen from the dead. The Son of God is risen as He said. Let's sing a song of praise.

48 Festivals and Seasons

2. The Son of God appeared to Magdalen;
the Son of God appeared to Magdalen.
He went into the Holy City;
He went into the Holy City.
Simon disbelieved till he saw His glory;
Simon disbelieved till he saw His glory.

Chorus

3. The Son of God will come to earth again;
the Son of God will come to earth again.
He will judge us all with mercy;
He will judge us all with mercy.
In heav'n the good will live for eternity;
in heav'n the good will live for eternity.

Chorus

Add a strong drumbeat in the chorus.

Festivals and Seasons 49

22 Holi with Shyam

Sujan Rawtani

At a moderate speed
Instrumental

Au - j khe - lo Shy - am sun - g Ho - ri Pi - ch - ka - ri ran - g bha - ri ke - sa - r kee. Au - j khe - lo Shy - am sun - g Ho - ri Pi - ch-ka-ri.

On this day let's play Ho - li with Shy - am. Saf - fron - filled sy - rin - ges are all here for us to spray. Let us to - day play Ho - li with Shy - am. What co - lour!

Instrumental

Kan - war Kan - hi - ya sun - g sak - hi Rad - ha Ran - g bha - ri jor - ri so - hat ree.

See, Prince Kan - hi - ya plays with his friend Rad - ha. Oh what love - ly co - lours! What a fine pair.

D.C.

50 Festivals and Seasons

Getting faster
Coda (sung after the repeat of the song)

Au - j khe - lo Shy - am sun - g khe - lo Shy -
Oh this day let's play Ho - li now, to - day play

am sun - g khe - lo Shy - am sun - g Ho - ri.
Ho - li now, to - day play Ho - li with Shy - am.

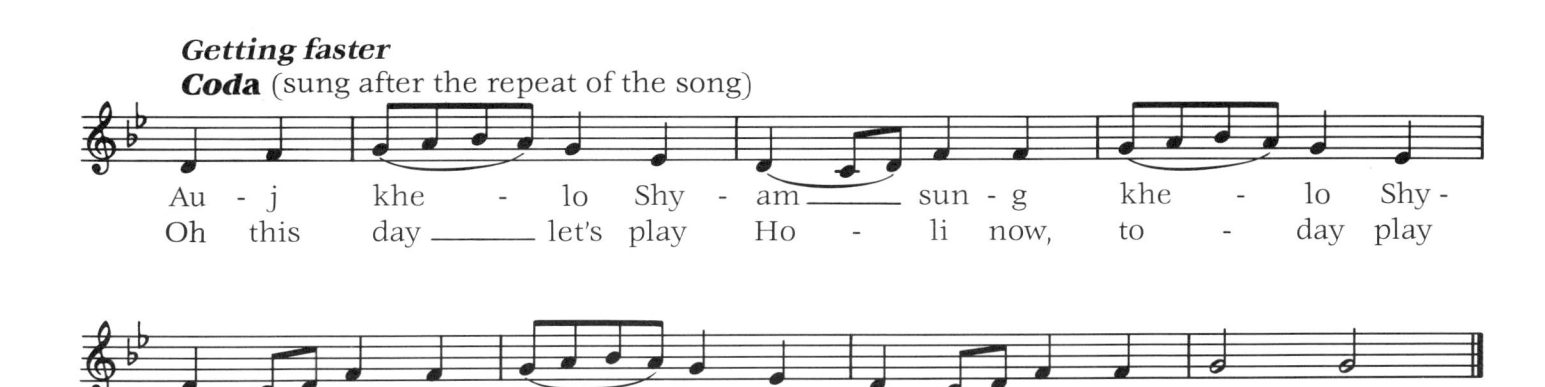

*You could use a contrasting rhythm on a tambour or any instrument you have available. The interludes were originally played on the harmonium, which also doubled the line of the singer. In the word setting some final consonants are sounded as a separate syllable with a separate note, for example sun**g**, ran**g**, kesa**r**.*

Holi

This carefree Hindu festival is celebrated in February/March, but comes at the end of the Hindu year. Some people think that the origin of the bonfire, which forms a central part of the celebration, is in the burning up of the year's accumulated rubbish. Another explanation lies in the legend of a demon, Hiranyakashipu, who tried to destroy his son, Pralhad, because he was a devotee of one of the Hindu gods, Vishnu. He tried having him trampled to death by an elephant, throwing him from a high mountain and drowning him in a river. But each time Pralhad was saved by his devotion to Vishnu. At last the demon tried burning him, but his sister Holikaa saved him although she perished in the flames. Whatever its origin, the bonfire is sacred and each family near the site must contribute to it; children even have the right to steal wood for it. People walk round the bonfire in reverence and then streak their foreheads with the ashes to bring good luck for the coming year.

The festival lasts three to five days with street dancing and processions and singing. People also remember the innocent frolics of the Hindu god Krishna with the merry milkmaids of Vrindaban and how cowherds and milkmaids sprayed each other with red powder. This is why, at Holi, metal or bamboo syringes are filled with red-coloured liquid or powder and used to spray friends and animals. After this the participants bathe and settle down to a feast of sweetmeats and vegetarian dishes.

The song refers to the spraying ceremony. Shyam and Kanhiya are names for Lord Krishna, and Radha is Lord Krishna's lover. Sujan Rawtani, who wrote the song, sees a deeper meaning in it than just merrymaking. He sees remembering God in a game and getting wet as becoming one with God and a part of His purity. The syringe full of *kesar* (saffron), which is a pure colour, represents having complete confidence in God. The unity of the couple Radha and Shyam–Radhashyam may also represent the uniting of the worshipper with God.

23 Phagun lege
Spring song

Rabindranath Tagore
Translated by Bhadra Patel

Gently

Pha-gun le-ge chhe bo-ne bo-ne O-re bai Pha-gun le-ge chhe bo-ne bo-ne
See how the spring is com-ing now in woods and fields! See how the spring is com-ing com-ing!

Da-le da-le phu-le phu-le Pa-tay pa-tay re a-ra-le a-ra-le ko-ne ko-ne.
On the branch-es, on the leaves are flo-wers and fruits now; see how spring is peep-ing round the cor-ner.

Pha-gun le-ge chhe bo-ne bo-ne O-re bai! Pha-gun le-ge chhe bo-ne bo-ne!
See how the spring is com-ing now in woods and fields! See how the spring is com-ing, com-ing!

Fine

Rong-e rong-e rong-i-lo a-kash ga-ne ga-ne ni-kh-il u-das.
See the sky is full of co-lours now; and i-mag-i-na-tion wan-ders free.

Ja-no cha-lo chan-chan-lo na-vo-pal-la-va-da-lo
Ev'-ry-thing is spring-ing up now; see the new leaves on branches!

Mo-r mo-re mo-r mo-ne mo-ne
How the mind is murm'ring with ex-cite-ment!

Festivals and Seasons

Pha-gun le-ge chhe bo-ne bo-ne O-re bai
See how the spring is com-ing now in woods and fields!

Pha-gun le-ge chhe bo-ne, bo-ne Ha-ro ha-ro a-bo-nir
See how the spring is com-ing, com-ing! See the earth is chan-ging its

ran - go ga-gon-e-r ka-re ta-po-
co - lour, And it casts its spell u-pon the

bhan - go. Ha-shi-r ag-ha-te tar
sky. See the laugh-ter and the per-fumes

mau-no ra-he-na aar Ke-pe ke-pe u-the kho-ne
ming-le to-ge-ther now; And it's spread a-round now by the

kho - ne. Ba-tash chhu-ti chhe bo-no moy - re
wind. See how the wind is gen-tly blow-ing

Phu-ler na ja-ne pa-ri choya - re. Tai bu-ji ba-re ba-re
O-ver the flo-wers ev'-ry-where now. At the ent-rance to the ar-bour

D.C. al Fine

kun-je ro da-re da-re Sud-hay phi-ri chhe jo-ne jo-ne.
o-ver and o-ver a-gain, Wind is an-noun-cing that the spring comes.

Festivals and Seasons 53

24 Padstow May Day song

Traditional English, arranged by June Tillman

Vigorously
Morning song

1. U-nite and u-nite and let us all u-nite, For summer is a-coming today, And whither we are going we will all u-nite, In the merry morning of May.

2. With a merry ring and with the joyful spring, For summer is a-coming today. How happy are the little birds which so merrily do sing, In the merry morning of May.

Chorus
Day song (unaccompanied)

Oh where is St George? O where is he now? He's down in his long boat all on the salt sea, O! Up flies the kite and down the lark, O! Aunt Ursula

54 Festivals and Seasons

Bird-wood she had an old ewe, And she died in the old park, O!

3. All out out of your beds. All out out of your beds.
   For summer is a-coming today.

   Your chamber shall be strewed with the white rose and the red,
   In the merry morning of May.

4. The young men of Padstow they might, if they would,
   For summer is a-coming today,
   They might have built a ship and gilded her with gold,
   In the merry morning of May.

5. The young women of Padstow they might, if they would,
   For summer is a-coming today,
   They might have made a garland with the white rose and the red,
   In the merry morning of May.

6. Where are the young men that here now should dance?
   For summer is a-coming today,
   Some they are in England, and some they are in France,
   In the merry morning of May.

Day song

7. Now fare you well and bid you all good cheer,
   For summer is a-coming today,
   We call no more unto your house before another year,
   In the merry morning of May.

Accompany the Morning Song with a drum on the first beat of each bar. The Day Song (sung slower and unaccompanied with pauses) is sung between verses 1 and 2 and 6 and 7. All other verses are sung to the Morning Song tune.

May Day

This song accompanies the May Day festivities at Padstow in Cornwall. The town is decorated and from midnight people sing the Morning Song round the streets. In the morning the two hobby horses (Obby Oss) – huge wooden frames with horse heads on top – set out round the town. During the Morning Song the Obby Oss prances and is 'teazed' or baited by a character called a Teazer. The Day Song is sung at intervals and the Oss 'dies'. On 'With a merry ring' he springs to life again.

The battle has been seen as having several meanings: the duel of winter and summer, St George and the dragon, Christian and the Devil, the sower and the Corn Spirit, and so on.

Festivals and Seasons

25 John Barleycorn

Steadily *Traditional English, arranged by June Tillman*

1 There came three men from out of the west, their fortunes for to try, And these three men made a solemn vow, John Barleycorn should die. They ploughed, they sowed, they harrowed him in, throwed clods upon his head, And these three men made a solemn vow, John Barleycorn was dead. 2 And

56 Festivals and Seasons

2   And there he lay for some little time till rains from heaven did fall,
    When little Sir John sprung up his head and that surprised them all.
    And there he stood till midsummer day and looked both pale and wan,
    And little Sir John grew a long, long beard and so became a man.

3   They hired men with scythes so sharp who cut him off at the knee;
    They rolled him and tied him by the waist and served him barbarously,
    They hired men with sharp pitchforks who pricked him to the heart,
    But the loader he served him worse than that for he tied him to the cart.

4   They wheeled him round and round the field till they came unto a barn,
    And there they made a solemn mow of poor John Barleycorn.
    They hired men with crabtree sticks, who cut him skin from bones,
    But the miller he served him worse than that, for he ground him between two stones.

5   There's little Sir John in the nut-brown bowl and he's brandy in the glass,
    And little Sir John in the nut-brown bowl proved the strongest man at last;
    For the huntsman he can't hunt the fox or so loudly blow his horn,
    And the tinker he can't mend the kettles and the pots without a little Barleycorn.

Accompany this with a drum on the first and third beats of the bar.

The legend of John Barleycorn

It has been suggested that the story of John Barleycorn embodies the ancient belief in a vegetation spirit killed for the sake of the fertility of the crops. A simpler explanation is that it is the story of barley from grain until it is fermented into an alcoholic drink. The song is sometimes called 'The Passion of the Corn'.

Festivals and Seasons

26 Buddha Lord we offer
Holy day of Wesak

Words by D. Hurst
Music: Temple chant

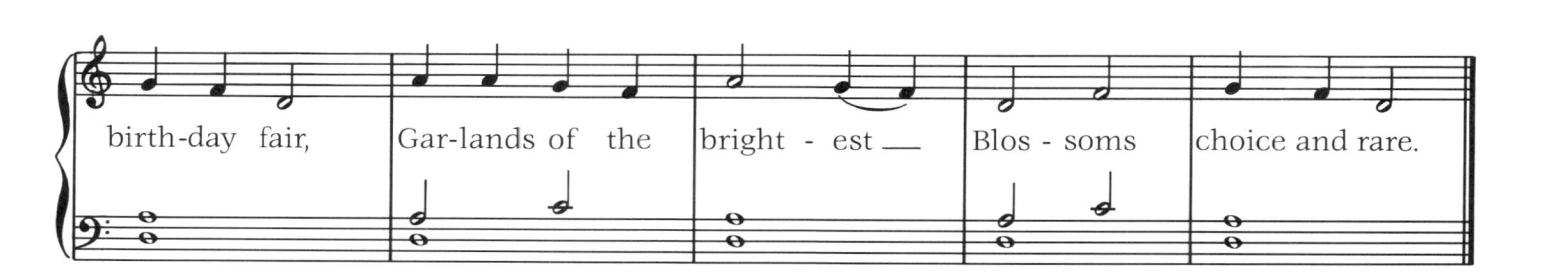

With dignity
Introduction

1 Buddha Lord we offer
  On Thy birthday fair,
  Garlands of the brightest
  Blossoms choice and rare.

2 Holy Day of Wesak,
  Day of Buddha's birth,
  When the sun of wisdom
  Shone upon the earth.

3 Incense too we offer
  On this Festal Day,
  For the things we cherish
  All must pass away.

4 Through this holy symbol,
  We shall learn to see,
  Things of priceless value
  Hid in transiency.

5 And the deep gong sounding
  Bids us leave the self,
  And in Buddha's teaching
  Find the truest wealth.

6 Lights upon the altar
  Show to us the way,
  From the realms of darkness
  To Nirvana's day.

Festivals and Seasons

Pitched Percussion

Recorders

Wesak

This is the main festival of Buddhism and in one tradition celebrates the birth, the enlightenment and the death of the founder of Buddhism, Gautama Buddha. He was the son of a North Indian ruler who searched for an answer to the problem of suffering. He found this while thinking beneath the Bo-tree or 'Tree of Enlightenment' and set out his ideas in a sermon in Benares. In this he spoke of the Four Noble Truths: that suffering is part of life which is caused by selfishness, and will end when selfishness is destroyed by means of the Eightfold Path (right understanding, right thought, right speech, right action, right vocation, right effort, right mindfulness, right concentration). By following this path the Buddhist believes that he or she will reach Nirvana – a state of bliss. Buddhists do not believe in or worship a creator god or gods. Monks play an important part in their tradition.

Wesak is a three-day festival with flower and lantern decorations and large processions. Candles are lit and birds released as a symbol of Buddha's compassion. Flowers are offered to the Buddha, presents are exchanged and gifts are made to the poor. People meditate together.

27 Avare varsad
Come, come, rain

Gujerati song collected from Habib Latif

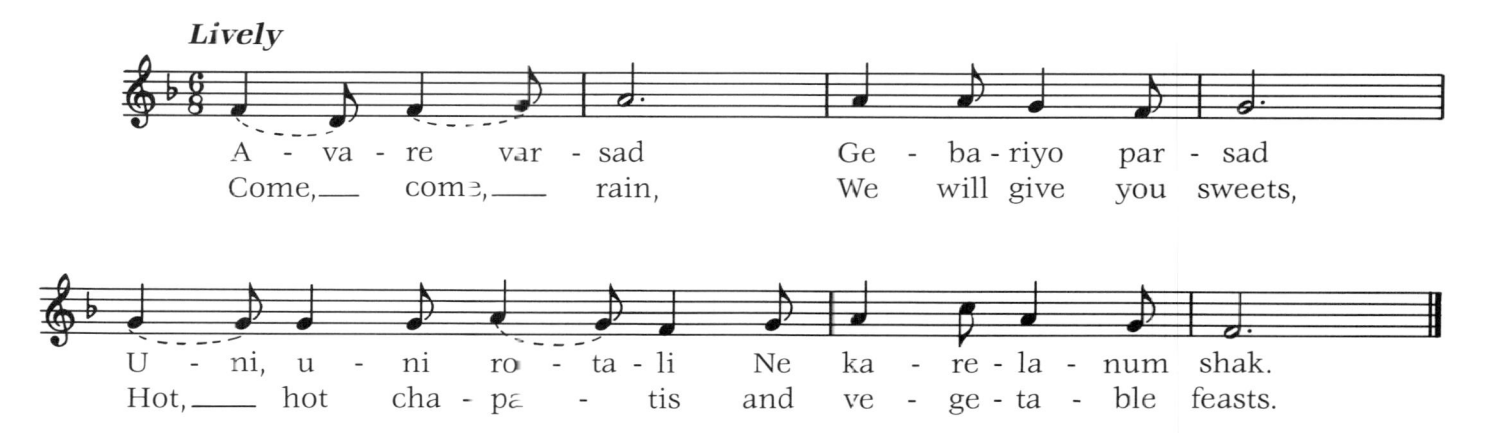

Lively

A - va - re var - sad Ge - ba - riyo par - sad
Come, come, rain, We will give you sweets,

U - ni, u - ni ro - ta - li Ne ka - re - la - num shak.
Hot, hot cha - pa - tis and ve - ge - ta - ble feasts.

Rain ceremonies

In hot countries there are many ceremonies in which people offer prayers to a god or gods for rain. The Indians in the Arizona desert filled themselves with cactus juice in the hope that the earth would be filled with rain. The Hopi Indians used a snake dance for the same purpose. Processions to a spring and the ceremonial pouring of water over the altar, form part of the Jewish festival of Sukkoth.

28 Aye re aye
Eid is here

Urdu song collected from Janki Sastry by Mary Plummer

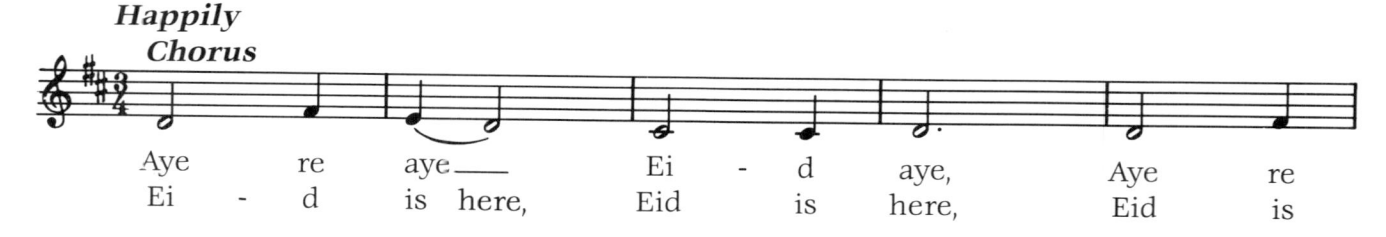

Happily
Chorus

Aye re aye Ei - d aye, Aye re
Ei - d is here, Eid is here, Eid is

60 Festivals and Seasons

[Music notation with lyrics:]

aye___ Ei - d aye. Ap - ne saath
here,___ Eid is here. Hap - pi - ness

Fine

khu - si - yan laa - yee Aye re aye___ Ei - d aye.
comes a - long with it. Eid is here,___ Eid is here.

Quick Verse

1 Ba - ji bhi aye___ thé Bha - ya bhi aye___ thé
 Our sis - ter came___ and our bro - ther al - so,

D.C. al Fine

Laa - ye thé mi - tha - ye yan Pa - ka - ye thé se - mi - yan.
They brought us sweets to eat and Al - so we cooked se - mi - yan.

2 Jhule bhi jhule thé
 Pehne the naaye kapre
 Amni khushi bash thi
 Abba bhi sath thé
 Chorus

2 How we were swinging,
 We had new clothes on,
 Mum was so happy that day,
 Dad was there with all of us.
 Chorus

Eid ul-Fitr

This Muslim festival marks the end of Ramadan, the month of fasting. During this month no food or drink may be taken during the hours of daylight, to remind Muslims what it feels like to be poor and hungry, as a commitment to God, and in obedience to His word in the Qu'ran. They also remember the giving of the Qu'ran and spend extra time in reading it and in prayer. Special foods are prepared, new clothes are worn, greetings and presents exchanged and houses are decorated. The day starts with special prayers and it is a time of reunions, settling old disputes and making a new start.

It is difficult to give even a rough idea when Muslim festivals are, because Muslims follow a lunar calendar – as do some of the other religions – which means that the festivals can occur in a different month each year.

Festivals and Seasons

29 Eid ul-Bukr

Mary Plummer

Happily
Capo 1st fret

Eid ul-Bukr, It's a happy festive day,
Eid Mubarak, It's the greeting that we say.
There'll be praying, there'll be feasting And our new clothes we will wear, We'll share the meat with one another Just to show how much we care.

You could use this song for Eid ul-Fitr by substituting 'the sweets' for 'the meat' in the verse.

Eid ul-Bukr or Eid ul-Adha

This festival is also known as the Festival of Sacrifice. It commemorates the time when Abraham agreed to sacrifice the first-born son to God but was released from this promise by God and sacrificed a ram instead. Now Muslims celebrate this festival by offering prayers at the mosque, re-affirming their faith in Islam, then sacrificing a lamb, goat, camel or cow; one-third is given to the poor, a third to their family and friends, and a third is for themselves. Friends are invited for dinner and greetings are sent during the four days of the festival.

Festivals and Seasons

Special Events

30 Lord of all hopefulness

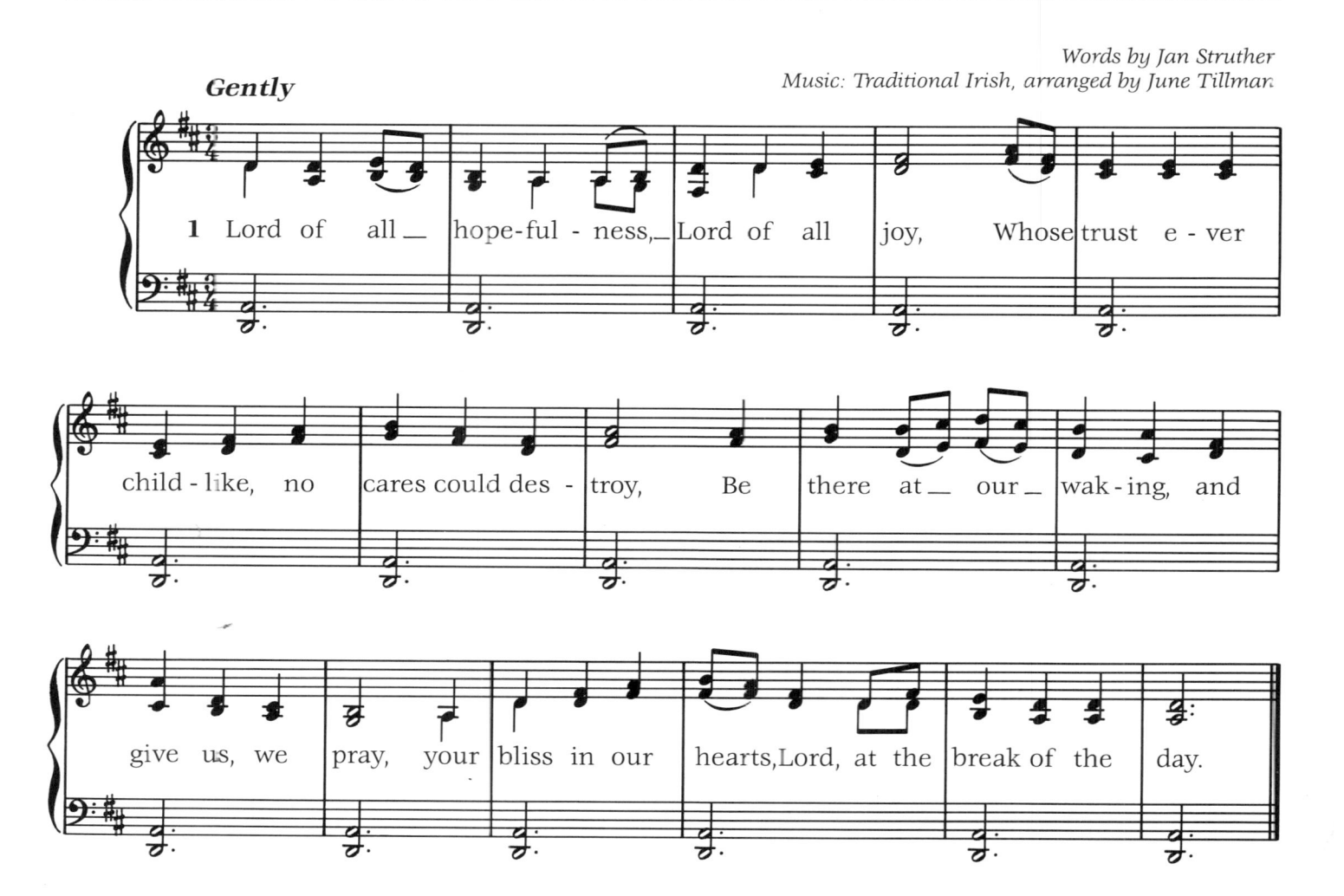

Words by Jan Struther
Music: Traditional Irish, arranged by June Tillman

1 Lord of all hopefulness, Lord of all joy,
Whose trust ever childlike, no cares could destroy,
Be there at our waking, and give us, we pray,
your bliss in our hearts, Lord, at the break of the day.

2 Lord of all eagerness, Lord of all faith,
Whose strong hands were skilled at the plane and the lathe,
Be there at our labours, and give us, we pray,
Your strength in our hearts, Lord, at the noon of the day.

3 Lord of all kindliness, Lord of all grace,
Your hands swift to welcome, your arms to embrace,
Be there at our homing, and give us, we pray,
Your love in our hearts, Lord, at the eve of the day.

4 Lord of all gentleness, Lord of all calm,
Whose voice is contentment, whose presence is balm,
Be there at our sleeping, and give us, we pray,
Your peace in our hearts, Lord, at the end of the day.

This Christian hymn asking for God's presence throughout the day
is set to a beautiful traditional Irish tune.

Special Events

31 Jabbin, Jabbin
Rise! Rise!

Traditional Australian Aboriginal

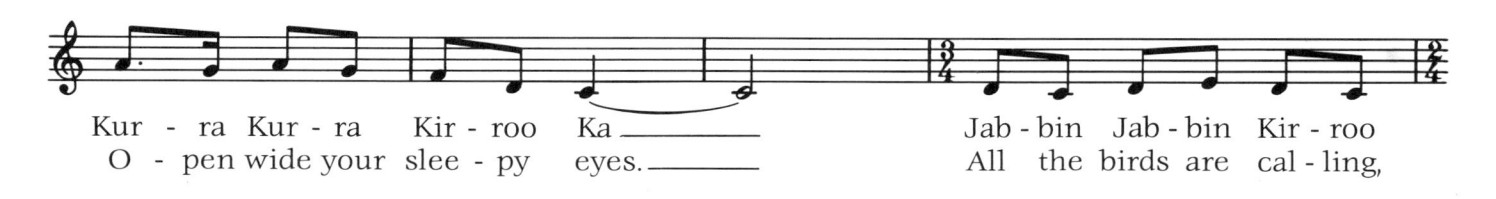

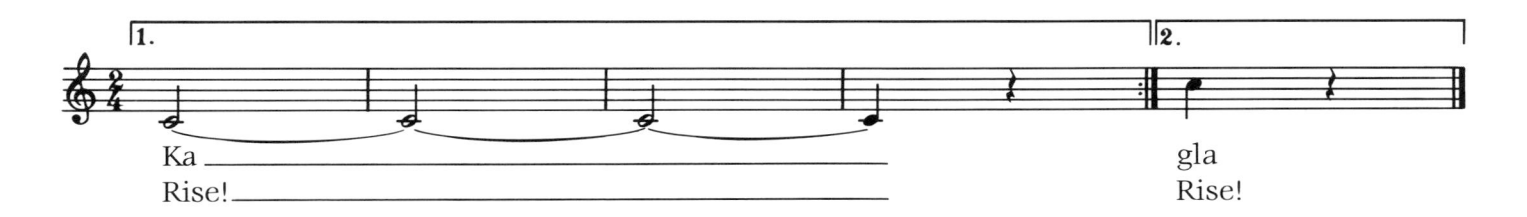

Gently swaying

Jab - bin Jab - bin Kir - roo Ka _____ gla
All the birds are cal - ling, Rise! _____ Rise!

Kur - ra Kur - ra Kir - roo Ka _____
O - pen wide your slee - py eyes. _____

Jab - bin Jab - bin Kir - roo
All the birds are cal - ling,

1.
Ka _____
Rise! _____

2.
gla
Rise!

*Pronounce the 'a' in 'Jabbin' as in **cat**, 'Ka' as in **path**, 'i' as in **lily** and 'u' as in **rug**.*

This is a pentatonic song and although the original was unaccompanied, you could invent accompaniments using

Aboriginal customs

The collector of this Australian waking song writes: 'Jabbin, Jabbin. . . is a song sung round the camp-fire. The aboriginals would be sitting on the ground and one of them would start. They would all join in singing the melody only, beating time with their hands or with boomerangs, and even at times an infant's tummy would serve as an impromptu drum!'

Special Events 65

# 32 Shabbat shalom

N. Frankel

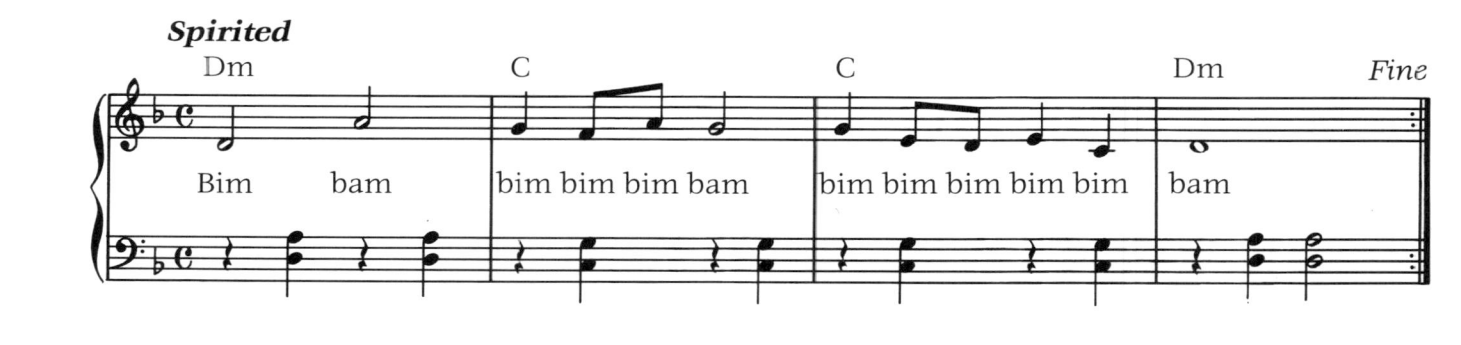

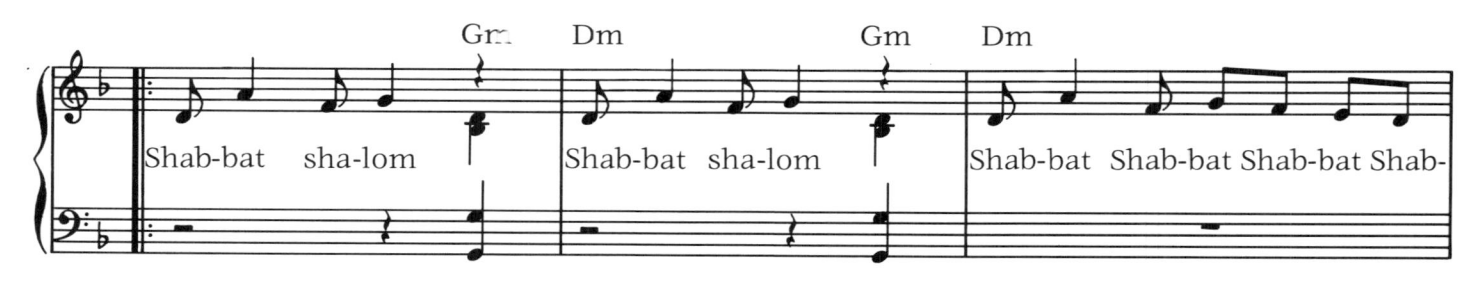

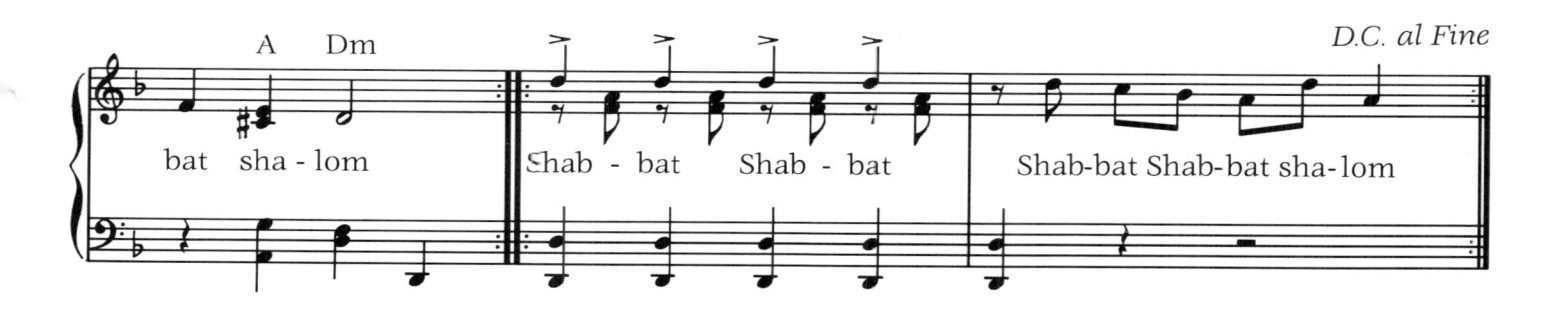

Spirited

Bim bam bim bim bim bam bim bim bim bim bim bam

Shab-bat sha-lom Shab-bat sha-lom Shab-bat Shab-bat Shab-bat Shab-bat sha-lom Shab-bat Shab-bat Shab-bat Shab-bat sha-lom

D.C. al Fine

'Shabbat shalom' means 'Welcome to the Sabbath'.

Descant Recorders

Shabbat (Sabbath)

The Jewish Sabbath begins every week on Friday evening with a joyful service in the synagogue. Afterwards there is a family meal. Everything must have been prepared beforehand, for no work can be done on the Sabbath.

The table is laid with a tablecloth and two candlesticks. There is a Kiddush cup of wine which reminds people of God's blessing of the *Shabbat*, his creation of the world and the freedom from slavery in Egypt. *Challoth*, twisted loaves with a special cover of white cloth, reminds them of the manna in the wilderness, and there are flowers, decorations and a book of blessings and songs.

Before the Shabbat Jews think about the successes and failures of the week gone by and put aside some money for the poor. During the meal the children are blessed and afterwards people talk, sing and tell stories. On the Saturday there are services in the synagogue and the whole festival ends with a blessing. Jews observe the Sabbath as a day of rest, recalling that, in the story of the creation of the world, God rested on the Sabbath day.

33 Hoya-hoye

We'll come again

Part 3 (see page opposite)
With vigour

Traditional Ethiopian, collected by E.L. Nelson

A - met lau - da - met, Di - ge - me - na. A - met Di - ge - me - na
Next year on this day, we'll come a-gain. Next year we'll come a-gain

Ye - ma - mi - yen bat-eh Di - ge - me - na, A - met Di - ge - me - na
In - to our mo-ther's house, we'll come a-gain. Next year we'll come a-gain

Ya - ba - bi - yen bat-eh Di - ge - me - na, A - met Di - ge - me - na.
In - to our fa-ther's house, we'll come a-gain, Next year, we'll come a-gain.

Pitched Percussion

×3

×3

(doubling L.H. of piano)

Descant Recorders

×3

68 Special Events

The song uses the pentatonic scale of

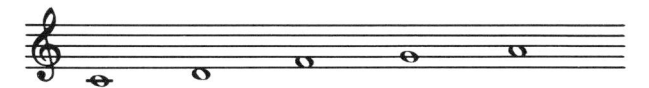

Make up more accompaniments using these notes.

The words 'our mother's house' and 'our father's house' refer to every house, for in Ethiopian villages every man was thought of as the father of the village children and every woman their mother.

Ethiopian New Year

The Ethiopian New Year falls on 11 September. After sunset on New Year's Eve, groups of small boys walk through their village carrying torches and serenading each house. Their song has three parts. In the first two parts of this version you chant the words. Here they are in Amharic, Ethiopia's official language. Pronounce them just the way they look, stressing each syllable equally.

Part 1

Hoya-hoye, hoya-hoye,	Hoya-hoye, hoya-hoye,
Yene mebet atiwhichi gwaro.	Mistress, don't go into your back-yard.
Ainish yaberal inde korkoro.	Your eyes shine like the sun from a tin roof.
Hoya-hoye, gude,	Hoya-hoye, I have a secret,
Dabo dabo yilal hode.	My tummy wants bread.
Ishim ahnd nuhw.	Yes is an answer.
Imbim ahnd nuhw.	No is also an answer.
Iguada gebto zimu mindinuhw.	But staying indoors in silence is no answer.
Hoya-hoye, gude,	Hoya-hoye, I have a secret,
Dabo dabo yilal hode.	My tummy wants bread.

The women of the house give the boys freshly baked bread and rolls after this first part. The leader of the boys thanks them in the second part:

Part 2

Weldew yikoyun kebdew,	When we come back a year from now,
Lamet wend lij weldew,	May you be blessed with a son,
Keguaro tija asrew,	And a calf tied in your back-yard,
Weldew yikoyun kebdew.	When we come back a year from now.

Part 3

All the boys sing the third part, which is a haunting song. The word *Digemena* repeats throughout the verse – it means 'once more'.

The letters A and B refer to two groups of singers. B sings *Digemena* in response to A.

Special Events

34 Kalo sile
Come, let us go

Traditional Nigerian (Ugabo tribe), collected from Victor Lawayin

Vigorously

1. E je-ha lo, e je-ha lo, ka-lo si le.
   Come, let us go, come, let us go in-to your house.

   O! O! O! O! E je-ha lo ka-lo, si le.
   Ah! Ah! Ah! Ah! Come, let us go in-to your house.

2. Make we go eat, make we go eat, please dear teacher.
   Ah! Ah! Ah! Ah!
   Make we go eat, please dear teacher.

Accompany this with drumming patterns, for example:

ka-lo si le

Festival food

Getting together and sharing a meal forms a part of most festivals. Special foods are often eaten, for example pancakes on Shrove Tuesday, turkey and pumpkin pie on Thanksgiving Day, latkes at Chanukah, or lamb at Pesach.

On some of these occasions special graces will be said. Some people say a grace before or after every meal. It is usually a brief thanks to God for providing the foods. Food also forms part of many acts of worship, for example the bread and wine in the Christian Eucharist, the *karah prasad* (a mixture of wheat flour, clarified butter or ghee, and sugar) of the Sikhs, and the *prasad* of the Hindus.

35 Salani

Farewell song

Traditional Malawian, arranged by June Tillman

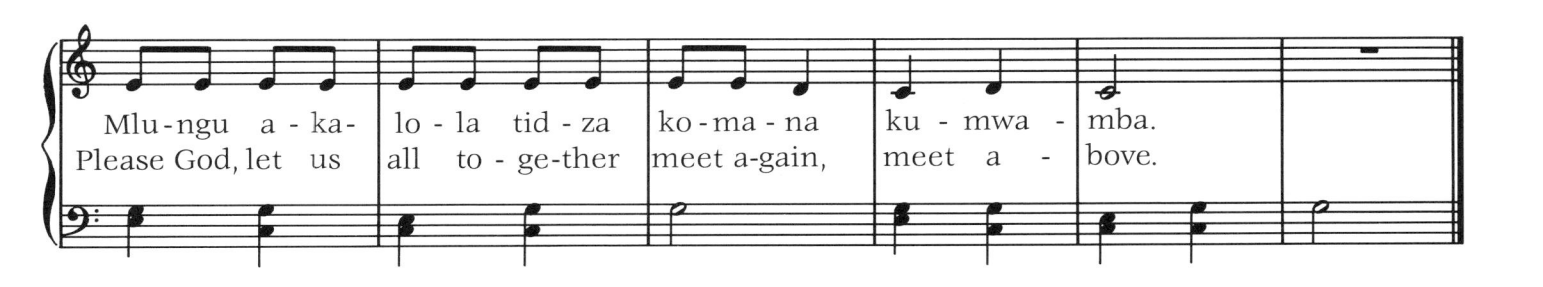

With dignity

Sa - la - ni Sa - la - ni e Sa - la - ni Sa - la - ni e
Fare-well now, may you fare well. Fare-well now, may you fare well.

Mlu-ngu a - ka- lo - la tid - za ko - ma - na ku - mwa - mba.
Please God, let us all to - ge - ther meet a-gain, meet a - bove.

Pronounce the 'a' long as in **path** *and the 'i' as* **ee**.

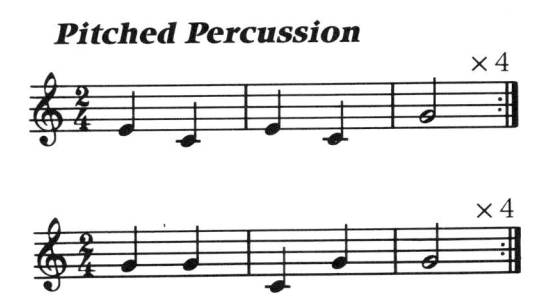

Pitched Percussion

×4

×4

Partings and farewells

Songs asking for a blessing on a parting are common to many religions. This one could be sung at the end of an assembly or at the end of a year. There are many stories of special farewells, for example the Last Supper in the Christian tradition.

36 Still now

Traditional Inuit, arranged by June Tillman

Gently

1 Still now and hear my sing-ing, Sleep through the night, my dar-ling. We have a ti-ny daugh-ter. Thanks be to God who sent her.

2 Though she as yet knows nothing,
   She is so sweet I'm singing.
   We have a tiny daughter,
   Thanks be to God who sent her.

This traditional Inuit (Eskimo) song is based on the pentatonic scale:

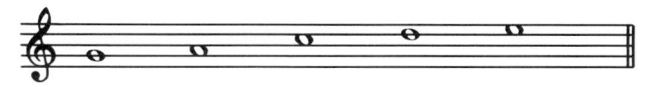

Make up some more accompaniments using these notes.

Pitched Percussion

Descant Recorders

Birth and naming ceremonies

The arrival of a new baby is always something to celebrate. In some countries a son is especially important because he will keep the family name alive and one day be head of the family.

Various religions have special ceremonies introducing the baby to the religious community in which he or she will grow up. Some Christian parents take their children to a church to be baptised, christened or dedicated. Not only is the baby named, but God is thanked and parents promise to bring the child up in the Christian faith. A Muslim father on the seventh day after birth names the child and whispers two calls to prayer in the baby's ear; then the first chapter of the Qu'ran is recited and prayers offered. Muslim male children are often called Muhammad, or babies are named after a member of the Prophet's family.

Sikh parents take their babies to their temple and present them before the Guru Granth Sahib (the Sikh holy book). The baby and the mother are given a mixture of sweetened water, called *amrit*, and verses from a holy poem are read. So, early in their lives the babies hear words which the parents hope will have deep significance for them. The Sikhs are named in this ceremony too. The holy book is opened at random and the first letter of the hymn on that page is declared to be the initial letter of the name.

A Jewish boy is circumcised on the eighth day of his life in accordance with their scriptures. Muslim boys are also circumcised. Hindus have an important ceremony when a priest gives the baby its name and offers prayers. Many of these ceremonies are followed by a family feast.

Special Events

37 Somagwaza
Initiation song

Traditional Zulu, collected by R.T. Abrams

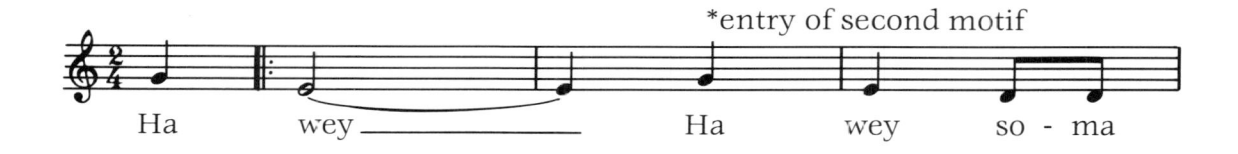

First motif

Ha wey ___ Ha wey so - ma gwa - za ___ Ha

*entry of second motif

Second motif

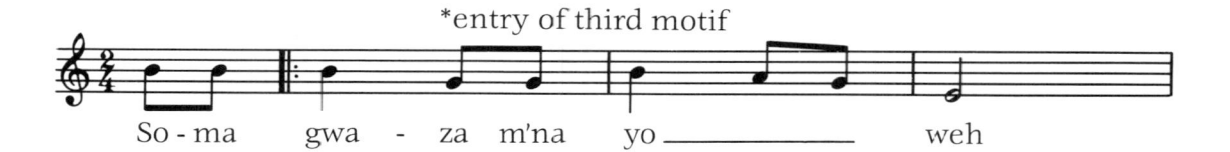

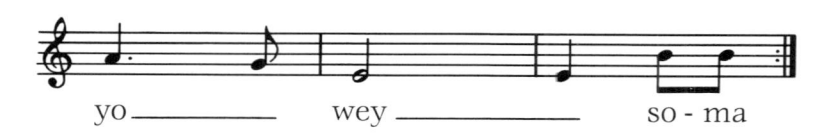

So - ma gwa - za m'na yo ___ weh yo ___ wey ___ so - ma

*entry of third motif

Third motif

Hey m'na yo ___ weh Hey m'na yo ___ wek so - ma gwa - za ___ Hey m'na

74 Special Events

Drum parts should be improvised but here are two suggestions for basic rhythms. Add further percussion as you wish.

Drums

Pitched Percussion (marimba or bass xylophone)
Notes for extemporisation:

This song is a traditional Zulu initiation song.

Initiation rites

Initiation rites are present in many world religions. In Judaism the initiation ceremony is known as Bar Mitzvah and it takes place when a boy reaches 13 years of age. He will read from the Torah (the first part of the Jewish holy book) and go through certain ceremonies in the synagogue as well as receiving a special blessing from the rabbi.

Sikhs have the Amrit ceremony when the boy or girl is sprinkled with *amrit* (sweetened water), and hymns and poems from the Gurus are read. After it the young person wears the five symbols of the Sikh faith, and a boy will wear a turban. Zoroastrians also give the young person a symbol – a girdle of 72 strands of lamb's wool representing the 72 chapters of their prayer book.

Christians of some traditions have a ceremony called Confirmation in which the bishop lays his hands on the young person's head and prays for the Holy Spirit to enter that person. Other traditions practise baptism of adults, which is often by total immersion of the person in the water.

38 Hey Motswala

Collected by R.T. Abrams

With vigour

Solo (or small group)

1 My mamma travelled to Pretoria to sign the licence for our wedding day. My mamma travelled to Pretoria to sign the licence for our wedding day.

Chorus (in 3 parts)

A, B Hey motswala, Hey motswala,
C   Hey motswala, ali wey, Hey motswala,

Hey motswala, Hey motswala.
Hey motswala, ali wey, Hey motswala.

(piano)

76 Special Events

2 My father wants to give the bride away.
   I think he's waiting for the dowry.
   (*Repeat*)
   Chorus

3 And now the time has come, I have to go.
   I wish perhaps I hadn't hurried so.
   (*Repeat*)
   Chorus

Accompany this with timpani doubling the left hand of the piano, and claves playing the following pattern during the verse but not in the chorus:

This Bantu wedding song has been used in many countries, including the USA where it was used as an advertising jingle on commercial radio.

39 Arabic wedding chant

Traditional Jordanian

Solo: Ah ya la-la-li, ya la-la-li.
Chorus: Ah ya la-la-li, ya la-la-li.

Solo: Ah ya la-la-li sah-ra li sit-ti,
Chorus: Ah ya la-la-li, ya la-la-li.

Solo: Ah ya la-la-li sah-ra li Manwey.
Chorus: Ah ya la-la-li, ya la-la-li.

Solo: Ah ya la-la-li a-rû-si Hel-wey.
Chorus: Ah ya la-la-li, ya la-la-li.

Solo: Ah ya la-la-li, ah ya la-la-li.
Chorus: Ah ya la-la-li, ah ya la-la-li.

Repeat the five stanzas two or three times then, when reaching stanza 5 for the last time, all join in repeating it six times, each time getting louder and faster.

'a' = **ah**   'i' = **ee**

Wedding ceremonies

Wedding ceremonies vary in different traditions. Christian and Jewish brides in the West wear white as a sign of purity. The Jewish ceremony takes place under a canopy and rings are exchanged, as in the Christian tradition.

Sikh brides wear red embroidered with gold, and the ceremony is held in the presence of their holy book, the Guru Granth Sahib. The bride's father puts a garland of flowers on this, and one on both the bride and groom.

At Hindu weddings the couple take seven steps together round a holy fire, making promises at each step. No official is present at a Muslim wedding, but two adults must be there as witnesses. They see the marriage as a contract made before God and other people.

Nowadays in Britain many people prefer to be married in the presence of the civil registrar and have no religious ceremony.

78 Special Events

40 Allah ju main
I am all alone

Punjabi song collected by Mary Plummer

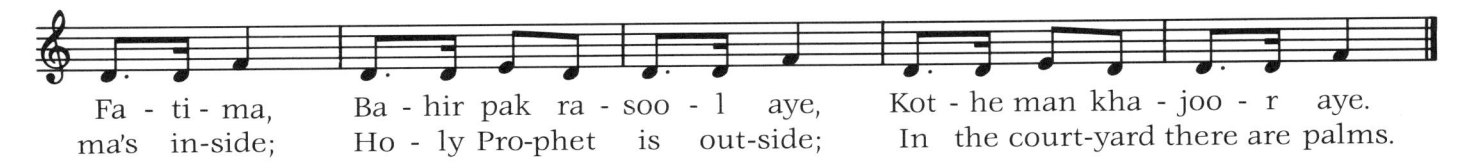

Steadily

Al - lah ju main a - kal - li hoon, Shehr Ma - di - né chal - li - hoon,
I am all a - lone, O God. To Me - di - na I shall go,

Shehr Ma - di - na doo - r aye, Ja - na bhi za - roo - r aye, An - dar Bi - bi
But the town is far a - way; But I will get there some - how. Bi - bi Fa - ti -

Fa - ti - ma, Ba - hir pak ra - soo - l aye, Kot - he man kha - joo - r aye.
ma's in - side; Ho - ly Pro - phet is out - side; In the court - yard there are palms.

Some final consonants are sounded as separate syllables, for example, 'door' = 'dooru' ('u' as in urn), 'bhizaroor' = 'bhizarooru'.

Pilgrimages

Devout Muslims are required to make a pilgrimage (*hajj*) to Makka once in their lifetime; Makka is Muhammad's birthplace and their holy city. The pilgrims wear special clothing to go into the mosque containing the Kaaba, a large structure with a black stone in its side said to have been built by Abraham. Seven times they move round it and kiss it. On the ninth day they go to the desert of Arafat where Muslims believe everyone will go on Judgement Day. There the pilgrims pray and make resolutions to improve their lives. After this comes the ceremony of Stoning the Devil at Mina.

After Makka pilgrims are encouraged to go to Medina to commemorate Muhammad's flight to that city. They should stay there long enough to say 40 prayers – about eight days.

The idea of pilgrimage is found in many religions, although its significance is different in different religions. For example, Christians go to places like the tomb of St Thomas à Becket at Canterbury or to Lourdes, where they hope to be cured of illness. Hindus go to the river Ganges and to temple festivals like the one at Puri in honour of Jagannatha, the 'Lord of the Universe' (a title applied to Vishnu and Krishna). Buddhists go to visit a footprint in a stone (the Lord's Foot), which is said to be that of the Buddha. Jews make pilgrimages to Jerusalem and Sikhs visit places associated with the Gurus. In Japan many people flock to Fuji-yama, the sacred mountain which is said to be the home of a goddess.

41 A Lyke Wake dirge

Collected by Hans Fried from Peggy Richards

Mysteriously

1 This ae nicht, this ae nicht, Ev'ry nicht and all, Fire and fleet and candle licht And Christ receive thy soul.

2 When thou from hence away dost pass,
Ev'ry nicht and all,
To Brig o' Dread thou com'st at last
And Christ receive thy soul.

3 When thou from hence away dost pass,
Ev'ry nicht and all,
To Purgatory fire thou cam'st at last
And Christ receive thy soul.

4 If e'er thou gavest meat or drink,
Ev'ry nicht and all,
The fire will never make thee shrink
And Christ receive thy soul.

5 But if meat or drink thou ne'er gav'st nane,
Ev'ry nicht and all,
The fire will burn thee to the bare bane
And Christ receive thy soul.

6 As verse 1

Pitched Percussion

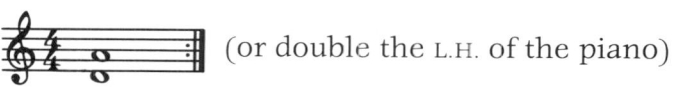

(or double the L.H. of the piano)

Judgement and life after death

A wake was originally an all-night vigil before a festival in a Christian church. It was a night of prayer, followed by the Eucharist. The idea of judgement is central to several traditions, especially Judaism, Islam and Christianity. This song goes through some of the ideas in the Christian tradition that make up the journey of the soul after death. Other ideas, too, are common to different religions, for example compassion, mercy and forgiveness.

Special Events

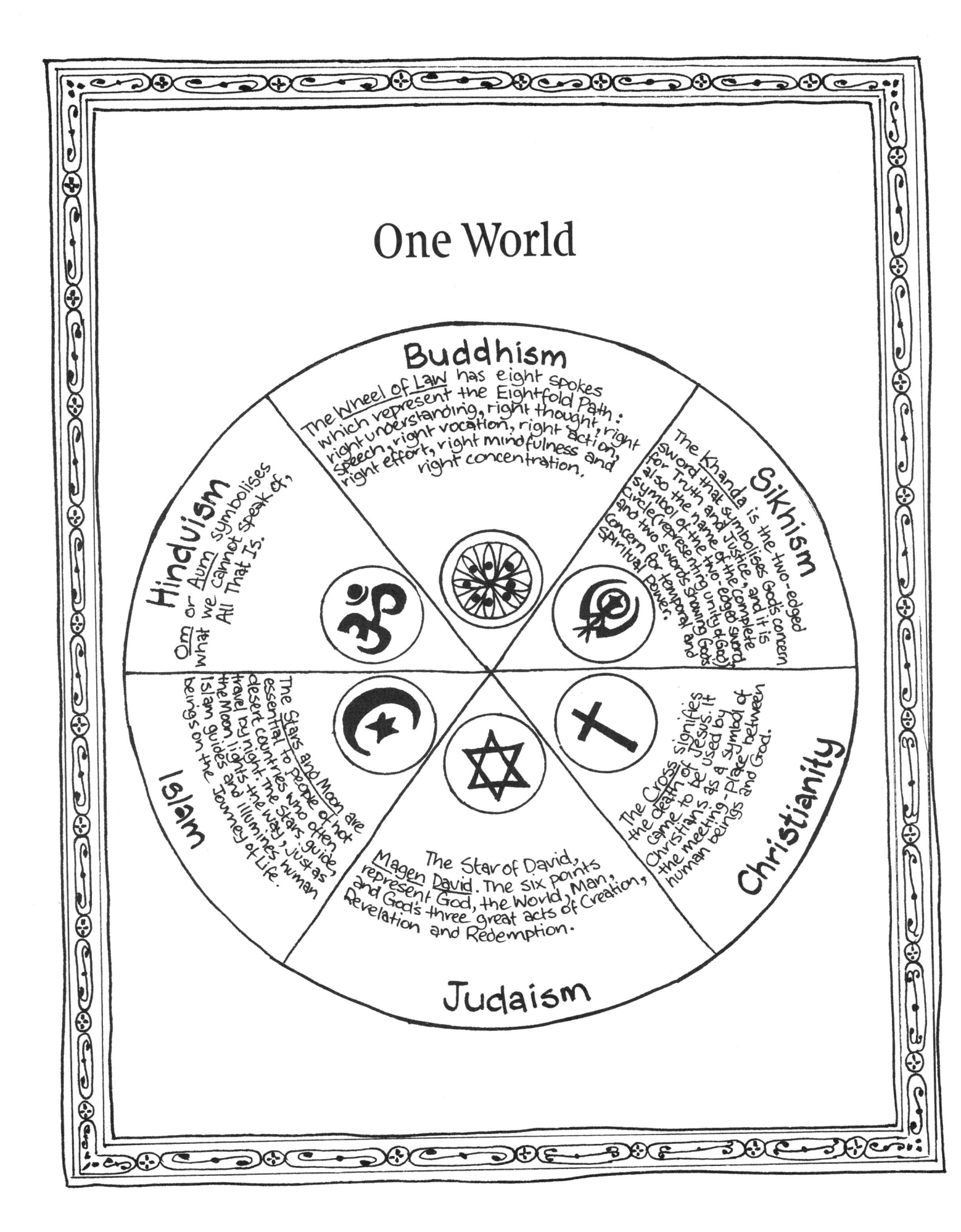

One World

Buddhism
The Wheel of Law has eight spokes which represent the Eightfold Path: right understanding, right thought, right speech, right vocation, right action, right effort, right mindfulness and right concentration.

Sikhism
The Khanda is the two-edged sword that symbolises God's concern for Truth and Justice, and it is also the name of the two-edged sword. Circle (representing unity of God) and two swords showing God's concern for temporal and spiritual power.

Hinduism
Om or Aum symbolises Brahm we cannot speak of, All That IS.

Islam
The Stars and Moon are essential to people of hot desert countries who often travel by night. The Stars guide, the Moon lights the way, just as Islam guides and illumines human beings on the Journey of Life.

Judaism
The Star of David, Magen David. The six points represent God, the World, Man, and God's three great acts of Creation, Revelation and Redemption.

Christianity
The Cross signifies the death of Jesus. It came to be used by Christians as a symbol of the meeting-place between human beings and God.

42 One world

Flowing   Capo on 3rd fret   R.W. Tysoe

Verse

1. It's the springs up in the mountains make the rivers of the plain, That bring water to the cities as they seek the sea again, And the rivers fill the oceans and the oceans make the rain, By the winds blowing over one world.

Chorus

And folk become our neighbours or our family or

2. There are people in the mountains and the valleys down below;
   There are people in the tropics there are people in the snow,
   Some are happy, some are homeless folk who have no place to go,
   But we all have to live in one world.
   Chorus

3. There are workers for their wages out in field and factory,
   There are fishers for our food supply in boats upon the sea;
   There are people still imprisoned in the cage of poverty
   As we labour for life in one world.
   Chorus

4. As the sun lights up the morning, and another day is found,
   It's a gift to all that's living, that the world still spins around,
   And the night is still the day but seen the other way around,
   As the sun shines upon this one world.
   Chorus

This song paints a broad canvas of the activities and resources of the world's people. Understanding each other 'depends on just where you stand'.

43 The world is dark

Gently
Capo 1st fret

Punita Perinperaja

Instrumental

Verse

1. The world is dark, we need the light, So give your love to make it bright. We need our friends kind,
2. The world is white, ma-ny peo-ple meet, If you are they will you greet. The years roll by;

Dm/C♯mi
till _ jour-ney's end, So hold my hand, if you're my friend.
these trea-sures you gain, Kind-ness my friend is not in vain.
Instrumental interlude
C7/B7
F/E
C/B
F/E
Chorus
F/E
Ev'-ry-bo - dy come on be a friend of ___ mine,
B♭/A
C7/B7
Hap-pi-ness is some-thing that's tru - ly di - vine.
F/E
Ev' - ry time you're an - gry _ try and cast it a - way,
C/B
Friend-ship and

kind-ness at work and at play.

Chime Bars
Verse

Chorus

This song was originally written for Diwali, but symbols involving light are common to many traditions. The Christian church uses candles in many ways. The song sets out the ideal of friendship between all races.

One World

44 ɔdɔ N'eye
Love your neighbour

Traditional Ghanaian, collected by Amoafi Kwapong

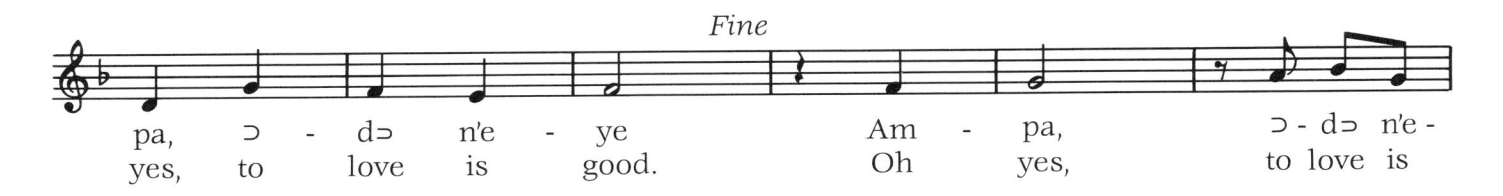

Steadily

Ao o - ni - pa da - sa - ni dɔ wo yɔn - ko se wo ho Am -
O all peo - ple on the earth, love your neigh-bour as your - self, Oh

Fine

pa, ɔ - dɔ n'e - ye Am - pa, ɔ - dɔ n'e -
yes, to love is good. Oh yes, to love is

D.C. al Fine

ye Am - pa ɔ - dɔ n'e - ye.
good, Oh yes, to love is good.

'ɔ' is pronounced 'o' as in **pot**. This is the Twi language of the Akan people of Ghana. It is a song for marching to, popular in the Presbyterian Church of Ghana. Accompany it with a drum in the rhythm:

One World

45 Nkosi sikelel'i Afrika
Bless our country

Enoch Sontonga

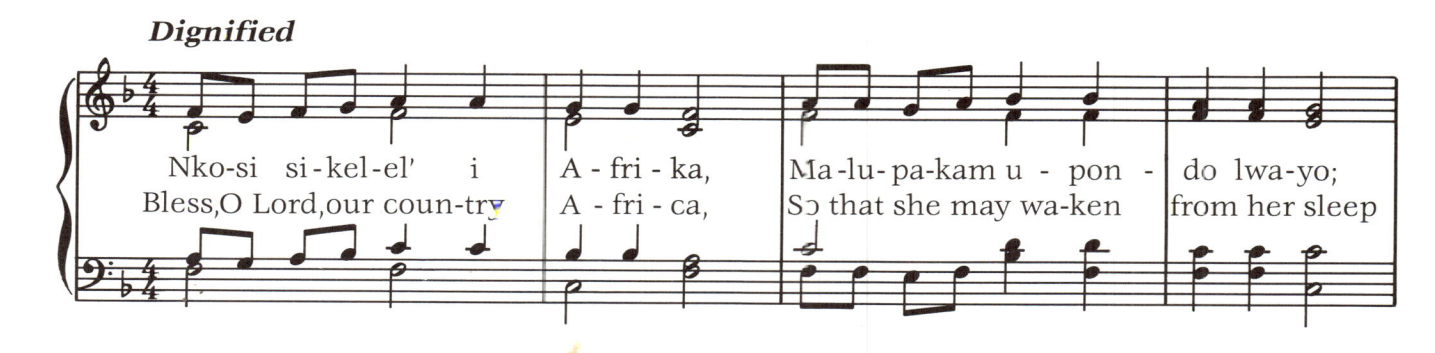

Dignified

Nko-si si-kel-el' i A-fri-ka, Ma-lu-pa-kam u-pon-do lwa-yo;
Bless, O Lord, our coun-try A-fri-ca, So that she may wa-ken from her sleep

Yi-va i-mi-tan-da-zo ye-tu. U-si- si-kel-el - e,
Fill her horn with plen-ty, guide her feet. Please, Lord, li-sten to our prayer.

U-si- si-kel-el - e *Fine* **Leader** Yih-la Mo-ya, **Chorus** Yih-la Mo-ya, **Leader** Yih-la Mo-ya,
Please, Lord, li-sten to our prayer. Spi-rit, de-scend, Spi-rit, Spi-rit, Spi-rit de-scend,

One World

D.S. al Fine

Chorus

Yih - la Mo - ya, Yih - la Mo - ya, O - ying - cwel - e.
Spi - rit, Spi - rit, Spi - rit des-cend, Spi - rit di - vine.

This hymn, sometimes known as the Bantu national anthem, is widely sung in South Africa. It was composed in 1897 by Enoch Sontonga, a teacher in one of the Methodist mission schools, who wrote many songs for his pupils but did not live to see them printed.

46 Buddhist blessings

Words by Koddaka-Patha and Sutta Nipa
Music by Colin Hodgetts

1 To forsake the foolish and follow the wise;
to honour those worthy of honour,
this is the greatest blessing.

2 Education, insight, control of oneself,
   to speak to the heart of the moment –
   this is the greatest blessing.

3 To live rightly, helping one's neighbours and friends,
   to follow a peaceful vocation –
   this is the greatest blessing.

4 To be meek, long-suffering, hating all wrong,
   untiring in works of compassion –
   this is the greatest blessing.

5 To be patient under correction, and meek,
   to act in full love with true virtue –
   this is the greatest blessing.

6 To be humble, reverent, grateful, content,
   to temper desire for a pure heart –
   this is the greatest blessing.

7 To lead simple lives in a beautiful land,
   reflecting on selfless examples –
   this is the greatest blessing.

8 To possess a heart unperturbed by the world,
   untroubled by grief or deep passion –
   this is the greatest blessing.

9 Those who act like this never suffer defeat,
   all roads they may travel in safety –
   theirs is the greatest blessing.

See 'Buddha Lord we offer', page 58.

47 Like a beautiful journey

At a moderate speed

Traditional Indian

1. Like a beau-ti-ful jour-ney is life. ___ No one knows what will hap-pen to mor-row. ___

La la ra la la ra la la, La la ra la la ra la, La la ra la la ra la la, La la ra la la ra la. Sing a-long, dance a-long, al-ways walk ___ tall. There is no point ___ in wor-ry-ing at all.

2. Smile a while; love your life; no more sorrow.
   No one knows what will happen tomorrow.

Bongos

Woodblock

Many religions see life as a journey. There are different views about how the future is determined.

92 One World

Songs of Praise

Sita · Vishnu · Rama

48 Simple gifts

Traditional Shaker

Gently and not too fast

'Tis the gift to be sim-ple, 'tis the gift to be free, 'Tis the gift to come down where we ought to be, And when we find our-selves in the place just right 'Twill be in the val-ley of love and de-light. When true sim-pli-ci-ty is gained, To bow and to bend we shan't be a-shamed. To turn, turn will be our de-light 'Til by turn-ing, turn-ing we come round right.

94 Songs of Praise

Use the lower part of the treble stave as an alto part.

Descant Recorders or Pitched Percussion

The Shakers

The United Society of Believers in Christ's Second Appearing flourished in the United States in the late 18th and the early 19th centuries. Originally derived from a branch of radical English Quakers, they practised shaking, dancing, whirling, and singing in tongues, as part of their lively worship. Devoted to hard work, their communities flourished and contributed several valuable inventions such as the screw propeller and distinctive styles of architecture, furniture, handicrafts and songs and dances. Shaker farms were much admired and the sect was famous for its fair dealing. Shakers were celibate and therefore declined in the late 19th century.

49 Hevenu Shalom
Peace unto you

Traditional Israeli

Pitched Percussion

Hevenu Shalom means 'Peace unto you'. As a translation you could sing 'May there be peace to all people'.

50 Raghupati
Gandhi's favourite hymn

Words traditional (verse 2 by Gandhi)
Translated by Badra Patel and June Tillman
Music traditional

With dignity

1 Ra - ghu - pa - ti, Ra - gha - va Ra - ja ___ Ram, ___
King Ram of the Rha - gu ___ fa - mi - ly, ___
Pa - ti - t pa - va - n Si - ta - Ram: Si - ta - Ram jai - ya
You pu - ri - fy sin - ners Si - ta's ___ Ram. Hail to Si - ta, to
Si - ta - Ram, Pa - ti - t pa - van Si - ta - Ram.
Si - ta's Ram! You pu - ri - fy sin - ners, Si - ta's ___ Ram.

2 Ishware, Allah tere nam

Sabbe ko sanmati de Bhagavan
SitaRam jaiya SitaRam
Patit pavan SitaRam.

3 Some call you Ishware, some Allah,
O God give good thoughts to everyone.
Hail to Sita, to Sita's Ram,
You purify sinners, Sita's Ram.

*In some words the final consonant is sounded as a separate syllable, for example, pati***t** *and pava***n**.

This was the prayer song used by Mahatma Gandhi at his daily prayer meetings. Each line is sung first by the leader and then repeated by the congregation. The whole song is repeated many times and other verses have been added. The second one given here is by Gandhi.

The prayer song invokes the help of Rama, a reincarnation of Vishnu, preserver and God of Love. The story of Rama and his wife Sita is told in the epic poem *The Ramayana* and remembered at such festivals as Diwali and Dashara.

Songs of Praise

51 Into the future

Words translated from the German by June Tillman
Music by D. Shostakovich

Steadily

1. Set out in the cool of the morn-ing, Set out by the stream in the wind. Our cares fade a-way in-to no-thing, For hap-py we let our song ring. Wake up! Get up! The morn-ing bursts in-to fi-ery flames. Our land is go-ing

for - ward now to meet new days.

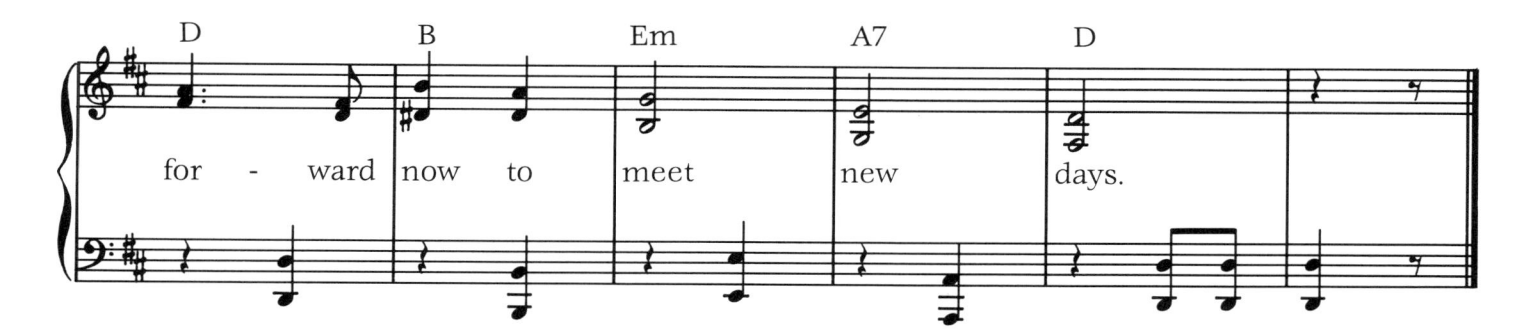

2 Forgotten are worry and suffering
And even work is easy now;
For ev'rything's seen with joy now;
We now see a better life.
For ev'rywhere we offer now the hand of brotherhood.
Chorus

3 Stand firmly! Our life is now conquered!
Courageously youth's going forth.
Our fathers began the work boldly
The victory now you complete.
Youth works and lives now as a symbol of victory.
Chorus

4 The song is now growing in splendour
Of beauty, of love and of light,
Of living when work does not damage,
Of bread that we'll have to the full.
In life and work we see the signs of happiness.
Chorus

The tune of this song was written by the Russian composer Dmitry Shostakovich, whose music was constantly under attack from the Soviet authorities until Stalin's death in 1953.

Communism

Communism is derived from the doctrines of Karl Marx in the 19th century. It calls upon workers to unite in a battle against capitalism in an attempt to create a classless society where all would be shared equally and with justice – 'From each according to his ability, to each according to his need'.

Communist governments have traditionally opposed religion, although some form of religion has struggled to survive under many of them.

Songs of Praise

52 Jon, jané, jana

Urdu song collected by Mary Plummer

Steadily

Sa - hib ne bu - l way a ha - zir hoon main a - ya,
The Mas-ter called and I re-plied, 'Sir, I am co - ming now.'

hoon ya roon ka main yar dush - man oon ka dush - man,
I am the friend of friends, and the e - ne-my of e - nemies.

Chorus

Dakh da - na da - n, jon ja - né ja-na da - n ta-ra rum pum pum pum pum,

Fine

jon ja - né ja-na da - n ta-ra rum pum pum pum pum.

Verse

Yeh ti - nu naam hain me - re yeh ti - nu
All of these names are mine, all of these

naam hain me - re Al - lah Je - sus
names are mine. Al - lah, Je - sus,

Ram hain me - re ji - s naam se jo cha - he jo-cha he muj-he bul-
Ram, all are mine. Any - bo - dy who wants me can call me by a - ny of

100 Songs of Praise

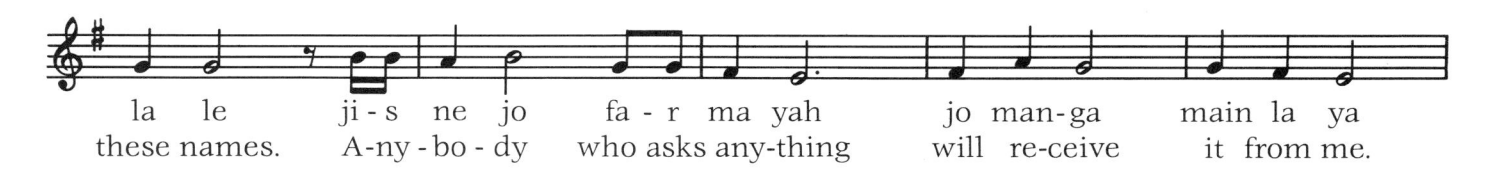

la le ji-s ne jo fa-r ma yah jo man-ga main la ya
these names. A-ny-bo-dy who asks any-thing will re-ceive it from me.

D.C. al Fine

hoon ya roon___ ka main ya dush-man oon___ ka___ dush-man.
I___ am the friend of friends, And the e-ne-my of e-ne-mies.

*Some final consonants are sounded as a separate syllable, for example, 'sahib' = sahibu ('u' as in **put**).*

Some people believe that all religions worship the same God, calling Him by different names. There is a story called 'The Blind Men and the Elephant' which illustrates this. This story can be found is several books, for example, *The Oxford Assembly Book*, published by *Oxford University Press* (1989).

53 Koee bolay Ram Ram
Some do call you Rama

Collected from the Sikh Gurdwara of South London

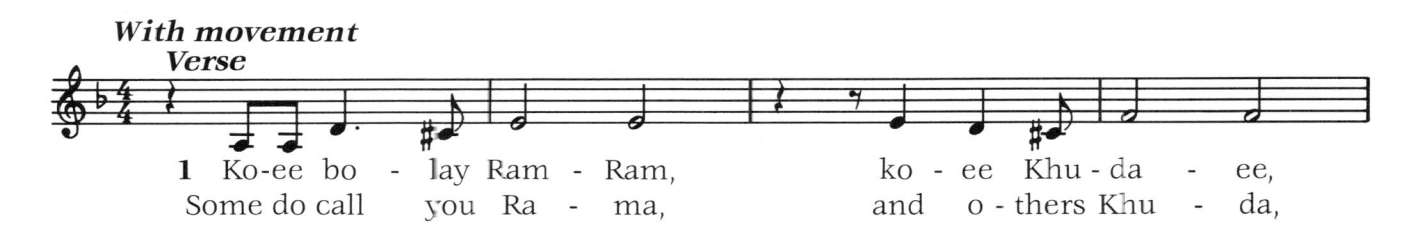

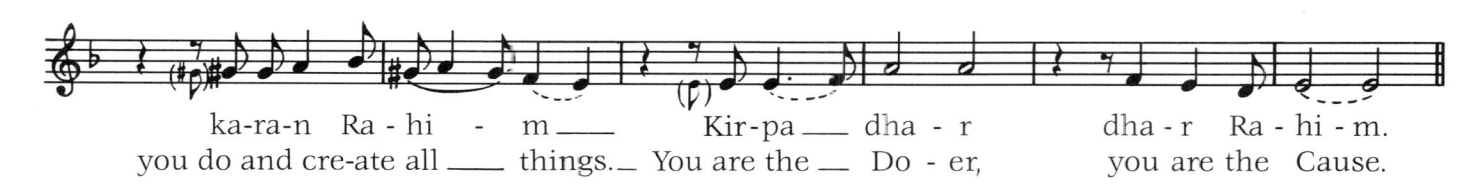

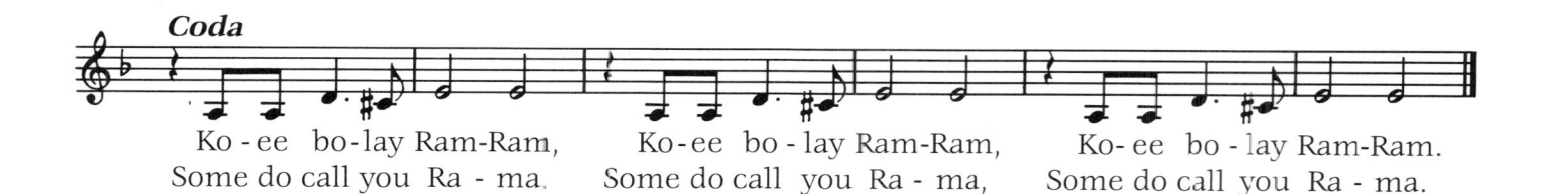

With movement
Verse

1 Ko-ee bo - lay Ram - Ram, ko - ee Khu - da - ee,
Some do call you Ra - ma, and o - thers Khu - da,

Last time to Coda

Ko - ee sa - vay Gu - saee - aa, ko - ee A - la - hay.
O - thers serve you as Go - sain, o - thers as Al - lah.

Instrumental **Chorus**

Kaa - ra - n
O most

ka - ra - n ka - ra - n Ra - hi - m Kaa - ra - n ka - ra - n
gra - cious Lord, you do and cre - ate all things. But, O most gra - cious Lord,

ka - ra - n Ra - hi - m Kir - pa dha - r dha - r Ra - hi - m.
you do and cre - ate all things. You are the Do - er, you are the Cause.

Coda

Ko - ee bo - lay Ram-Ram, Ko - ee bo - lay Ram-Ram, Ko - ee bo - lay Ram-Ram.
Some do call you Ra - ma. Some do call you Ra - ma, Some do call you Ra - ma.

2 Hindus go on pilgrimage, others will perform Hajj (*twice*)
   Some will bring you offerings, some bow before you.
   Chorus

3 Some will read the Vedas, others will read their holy books (*twice*),
   Some are robed in white robes, some like their blue robes.
   Chorus

4 Some of them are called Turks, others are called Hindus. (*twice*)
   Hindus seek for heaven, Muslims for Paradise.
   Chorus

5 But Nanak speaks now; He who knows the Lord's will (*twice*)
   Shall find the mystery of his Lord, the God.
   Chorus

   Coda

2 Koee navay teerath, koee hujj ja - ay (*twice*)
   Koee karay pooja, koee sir niva-ay
   Chorus

3 Koee parhay Bade, koee kitabay (*twice*)
   Koee odhay neel, koee sufade.
   Chorus

4 Koee kahaey Turk, koee kahaey Hindu (*twice*)
   Koee bacchay bahisht, koee sur gindu.
   Chorus

5 Koh Nanak jin hukam pachhata (*twice*)
   Prabh sahib ka tin bhade jata.
   Chorus

   Coda

Accompany this with bongos playing 4/4 ♪♪♪♪ ♪♪♪♪ :||

and a tambourine 4/4 ♩ ₹ ♩ ₹ :||

*The instrumental interlude that starts the verse is played on a harmonium, but use anything you have available. Some consonants are sounded as separate syllables, for example, 'Karan' = Karan***u** *('u' as in* **put***), 'Rahim' = Rahim***u**.

Songs of Praise 103

Sikhism

Sikhism is the name given to the teaching of Guru Nanak (1469–1538) and draws on Hinduism and Islam as well as Nanak's own teachings. He was followed by nine more Gurus, all regarded as perfect by the Sikhs, who see union with their Gurus as a way to salvation. The tenth Guru chose no successor, but instead saw the Guru Granth Sahib – a book in which the sayings of some of the Gurus and others have been recorded – as the source of all teaching after his death. This holy book is given a place of great importance in the *gurdwara* (the Sikh place of worship) and the hymn 'Some do call you Rama' is taken from it.

Sikhs have no priests, because they believe that all men are equal. At the end of an act of worship everyone shares *karah prasad* (a mixture of flour, butter and sugar) and then a meal in the kitchen (*langar*). Sikhs are initiated into the brotherhood which has certain rules including making vows to work for the community and giving part of its income for religious and social work. The turban is one of the signs of the brotherhood. The beliefs of Sikhism are summarised in the Mul Mantra, which, translated from the Punjabi, reads:

'There is one God. His name is Eternal Truth. He is the maker of all things and He lives in all things. He is without fear and without enmity. His image is timeless. He is not born: neither does He die to be born again. By the grace of the Guru, He is made known to men.'

The main Sikh festivals celebrate various events in the lives of the Gurus, the giving of the Guru Granth Sahib, Diwali and Holi.

54 Sanctus

Clemens non Papa
Unaccompanied round for five voices

Very smooth, at a moderate speed

A: Sanc - - - - - tus

B: Sanc - - - -

C: - tus Sanc - - -

D: —

E: - tus Sanc - tus

*each new voice enters here

'Sanctus' is the Latin name for the hymn 'Holy, holy, holy', which in Christian worship is sung before the Eucharist, the ceremony of bread and wine. This setting comes from Renaissance Italy.

55 Ruu tat
The heavens are speaking

Traditional Pawnee Indian

Dignified

1. Ruu tat lu ra we ri - ku Ruu tat lu ra we ri - ku Ruu tat ru ra we ri - ku we rix wa - wak ti ku he ris ta ki-ta-wi-u he he.

   As I stood be-neath the sky, As I stood be-neath the sky, As I stood be-neath the sky, See the clouds are speak-ing, I say You are the ru-ling po - wer.

2. I don't fully understand,
   I don't fully understand,
   I don't fully understand,
   You the ruling pow'r speaks,
   For the pow'r is yours, O you heavens.

Many religions see God in the natural world.

106 Songs of Praise

56 Ogun ba mi re
Song to Ogun

Traditional Yoruba, collected by Anthony King

With vigour

O-gun ba mi re me ba ma jao — ba mi re ma ba mi jao.

Start the drums first, one after the other, before the singing starts.

Drums

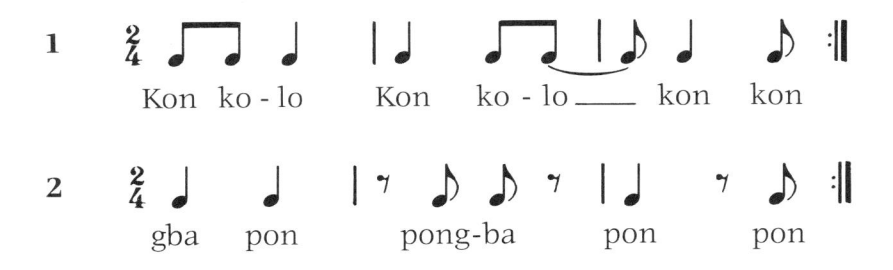

1. Kon ko-lo Kon ko-lo — kon kon

2. gba pon pong-ba pon pon

The story of Ogun

This is a simple prayer for the protection of Ogun, god of iron and war. It was used by hunters setting out into the bush. The translation runs:

SOLO: Ogun befriend me, don't fight me;
CHORUS: Befriend me, don't fight me.

Ogun is worshipped by blacksmiths, hunters and warriors and his festival takes place among the Yoruba in Ifaki, Nigeria, in September. The worshippers gather at the house of the chief priest, and guns and cutlasses are placed in a large circle laid out with young palm shoots, which are also tied on the bodies of the worshippers while they dance and drum. Three kola nuts are offered to Ogun and a dog is ritually sacrificed, the head being placed in the Ogun shrine and the rest distributed among the worshippers. The music for the merrymaking that follows is very vigorous and fierce, offering an outlet for the energy of the worshippers.

57 Onisango

Traditional Yoruba, collected by Anthony King

With strength

O - ni - san-go d'e-wa nu, ko he — O he mi - mo

Use the drums to accompany this: one in the rhythm of the left hand and the other:

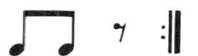

The god Sango

Sango is the god of thunder and lightning. He is said to have hanged himself from an ayon tree and a number of legends surround his death. One version is that he was a tyrant who, disheartened by the desertion of his wife, was dethroned and exiled by his opponents. His supporters, enraged by the slur cast on his name by his suicide, turned him into a god and said that he would use his power over thunder and lightning against anyone who spoke against his good name. They formed a cult to worship him with a chief priest known as the Baba mogba or chief advocate.

Sango's festival takes place around the end of July and beginning of August and lasts seven days. On the eve of the festival, worshippers and drummers dance, drink and feast at the expense of the Baba mogba. On the first day the drummers drum outside the Baba mogba's house in honour of Sango and collect money from him; they then proceed to the houses of other worshippers collecting money. On their way through the market they collect samples of local produce in a large basket or calabash. The contents are divided between drummers and the Baba mogba, who then has to return five-sixths of his share to the drummers.

Each day the drummers collect money from Baba mogba in return for playing in honour of Sango. But on the seventh day they receive only a large basket of *eko*, a type of solid maize porridge. During the course of the festival the Baba mogba will make offerings at the shrine of Sango, which is usually in his house. These will include: three kola, three *obi* (kola nuts), one cock, one white pigeon and one snail. Only the Baba mogba's family and the drummers will be present. During the ceremony the Baba mogba calls *kawo*, to which his family reply *kawo* ('O great and powerful Sango'), all this being accompanied by drumming.

The song means 'Should a Sango worshipper drop some beans (*solo*), don't pick them up or else you will pick up trouble' (*chorus*). One possible explanation of this is that in Sango worship the throwing away of beans is done as a protection against evil, as the beans are considered to contain hostile spirits.

Songs of Praise

58 Ruaumoko

Words by Ratu Tibble, adapted by June Tillman
Music by Sam Freedman

ra! He pe-ka nui ia koe, Ha
heav'ns as it goes flash-ing by He

ri-ri nui to ri-ri, he to-hu a-tu-a. E - nga-ri ko to
bright-ens up the hea-vens And ang-er is His cry. He strikes out like a

ra-kau, Tu-nga-we-re-we-re. Ka hi-ko ra!
wea-pon, His ang-er He sends out. The light-ning strikes,

Ma-na mo-tu-ha-ke i Wai-a-pu,
the ma-je-sty of a God from Wai-a-pu,

110   Songs of Praise

Many religions see God in the elements. In some myths thunder and lightning are seen as a god or gods being angry or having a battle.

Songs of Praise

59 Twameva

You are my mother

Sanskrit song collected from Bhadra Patel

With dignity

1. Twa - me - va ma - tu cha - pi - ta twa-me - va — Twa-me - va ban - du scha - sa - kha twa-me - va.

   My mo - ther you are and my fa - ther you are, — My bro - ther you are and my friend you are too.

2. Twameva vidya drawinam twameva
   Twameva sarvam mam deva dev.

2. My wisdom you are and my wealth you are too,
   For you are everything to me, O my Lord.

*The final consonant of 'dev' is sounded as a separate syllable: dev**e**.*

Deity worship

A Hindu might choose a deity to worship. The worshipper looks upon this deity as father, mother, friend, elder brother/sister, lover, husband/wife. Through this devotion the worshipper may obtain release from the cycle of birth and death, and good Karma. Karma is the belief that in the next incarnation a person will receive rewards or punishments in relation to their previous life on earth.

60 Shri Ram
Lord Ram

Traditional Hindi, collected from Bhadra Patel

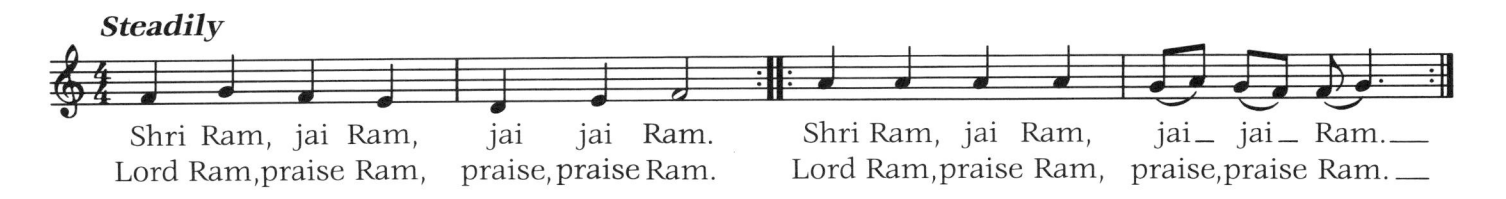

Steadily

Shri Ram, jai Ram, jai jai Ram. Shri Ram, jai Ram, jai jai Ram.
Lord Ram, praise Ram, praise, praise Ram. Lord Ram, praise Ram, praise, praise Ram.

This short chant is repeated by Hindus at many ceremonies. During funerals it may be sung for several days. It ends:

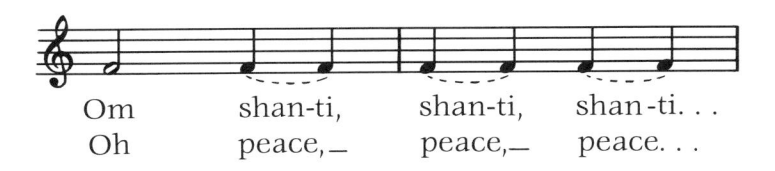

Om shan-ti, shan-ti, shan-ti...
Oh peace, peace, peace...

The story of Rama

Lord Ram or Rama is an incarnation of the god Vishnu. He is worshipped especially in northern India. His birth is celebrated at Rama Navami in March. His story is told in the epic poem *The Ramayana*, in which he is shown as appearing on earth to protect the good and the righteous from the forces of evil and to establish a new order amongst humanity.

The Hindu child is brought up to know the stories from the poem, and uttering the name of Rama is said to scare away evil spirits. The story of Rama and his wife Sita is remembered especially at Diwali and Durga, in September/October.

61 Hare Krishna
Praise Lord Krishna

Traditional Hindi, collected from Bhadra Patel

Ha - re Krish - na, Ha - re Krish - na, Krish - na, Krish - na, Ha - re, ha - re.
Praise Lord Krish-na, Praise Lord Krish-na, Krish-na, Krish-na, Praise Him, praise Him.

Ha - re Ra - ma, Ha - re Ra - ma, Ra - ma, Ra - ma, Ha - re, ha - re.
Praise Lord Ra - ma, Praise Lord Ra - ma, Ra - ma, Ra - ma, Praise Him, praise Him.

This is the traditional version of the chant.

Krishna

Krishna is a favourite deity of northern India, being an incarnation of Vishnu. His birthday, *Krishnashtami*, is celebrated in August/September at midnight when Hindus keep a vigil in the temple after 24 hours of fasting. Sometimes an image of Krishna is placed in a cradle along with sweets which are later eaten. There is singing and drama based on stories from the life of Krishna, taken from the Bhagavata Purana; many of these stories are told to Hindu children.

The story of Krishna's birth is very dramatic. He was born to Devaki, the sister of Kansa, who had usurped the throne. There was a prophecy that one of Devaki's eight children would kill their uncle, Kansa. So each time Devaki had a child Kansa smashed it to death. But although she was in prison when her eighth child, Krishna, was born, Devaki managed by a miracle to escape. The child – already demonstrating his magic powers – made the river divide and eventually they reached the house of a neighbour who then exchanged him for her own baby.

Devaki managed to return to the palace unnoticed and the neighbour's child was killed by Kansa while Krishna grew up safely. Kansa, who was told by a voice from heaven that Krishna lived, ordered all young children to be killed, but Krishna survived and destroyed Kansa. He established his capital, Dwarakaa, which is now a place of pilgrimage.

62 Let us praise Him

Black American spiritual

With strength

1. Let us praise Him, Let us praise Him, Glory, Hallelujah! Let us praise Him, O praise, O praise, Glory, Hallelujah!

2. I once was los' but now I am foun',
   Glory, Hallelujah!
   I once was los' but now I am foun'
   Glory, Hallelujah!

3. I never shall forget dat day,
   Glory, Hallelujah!
   When Jesus wash' my sins away,
   Glory, Hallelujah!

4. 'Twas little I thought He was so nigh,
   Glory, Hallelujah!
   He spoke and He made me laugh and cry,
   Glory, Hallelujah!

Pitched Percussion

This black spiritual from the United States of America contains many ideas found in the religious traditions of the deep south: being cleansed from sin, being lost and then found, and so on.

Songs of Praise

63 Carol of the creatures

Sydney Carter

Verses 1 and 7*
Free rhythm

1 Cre-a-tor high and ho-ly, To you all praise and power be-long, In all things liv-ing you are ca-rol-ing and leap-ing: You are the end and the be-gin-ning of their song. Oh,

Chorus
(a tempo)

Leap and ca-rol to the Lord, I say, Show what He has done, o-ho! Leap and ca-rol to the Lord, I say, And show Him like the sun. *Fine*

Verses 2–6, 8

2 And first I call my Bro-ther Sun For by that Light I see The

* *Verse 7 is sung unaccompanies to the tune of verse 1.*

Songs of Praise

(Repeat for vv. 3, 4, 5, 6 and 8)

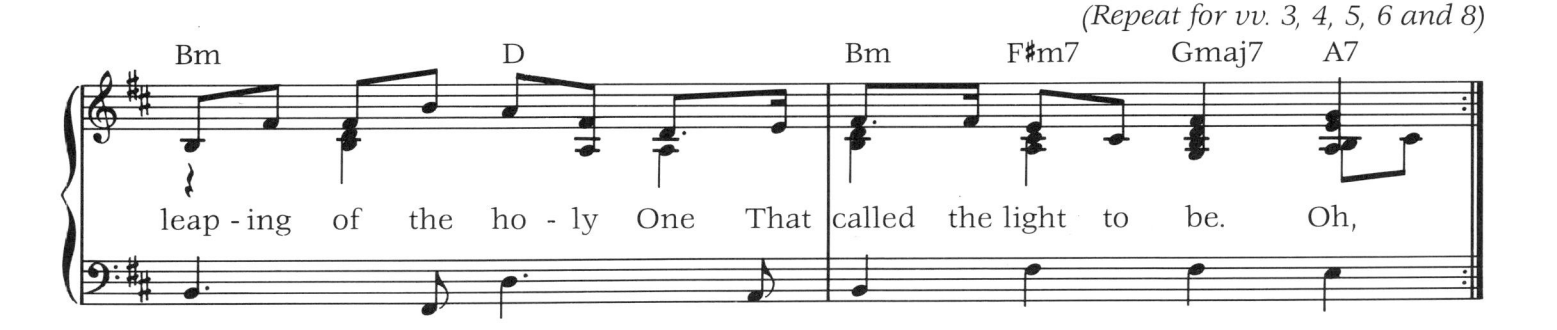

leap-ing of the ho-ly One That called the light to be. Oh,

3 I call upon my Sister Moon,
   I love that gentle light,
   And all the stars so sharp and clear
   That shiver in the night. Oh,
   Chorus

4 I call on you my Brother Wind,
   By weather foul or fair
   You show the likeness of the Lord
   I breathe Him like the air. Oh,
   Chorus

5 I call on you my Sister Water,
   Come down from the sky,
   And show the likeness of the Lord
   I drink Him or I die. Oh,
   Chorus

6 I call on you my Brother Fire,
   In yellow light and red
   You leap and carol to the Lord
   With sparks around your head. Oh,
   Chorus

7 My Sister Death you call me
   To leap and carol I cannot say 'no'.
   I am a dancer to the end and the beginning
   Of all the leaping and the carolling I go. Oh,
   Chorus

8 Come all you men and women too,
   Show pity and forgive.
   For by your love you show the Lord
   And with Him you shall live. Oh,
   Chorus

St Francis of Assisi

St Francis, who wrote the poem on which this is based, lived in the 13th century in Assisi in Italy. He gave up a life of riches in response to a heavenly voice. He preached about a life of poverty and giving all that you have to the poor. He gathered around him a group of companions, and founded an order of monks whom we now call Franciscans. St Francis, who wrote this beautiful song, is famous for his care for all God's creatures, including animals. The verse about death was sung while he was dying.

64 By the rivers of Babylon

Traditional, adapted by Dowe and McNaughton

Reggae

By the rivers of Ba-by-lon,— Where we sat down,

And there we wept,——— When we re-mem-bered Zi - on.—

Last time, fade...

But the wi-cked carried us a-way, cap-ti-vi-ty,— Re-qui-re from us a song.

How can we sing the Lord's own song in a strange

118   Songs of Praise

Songs of Praise   119

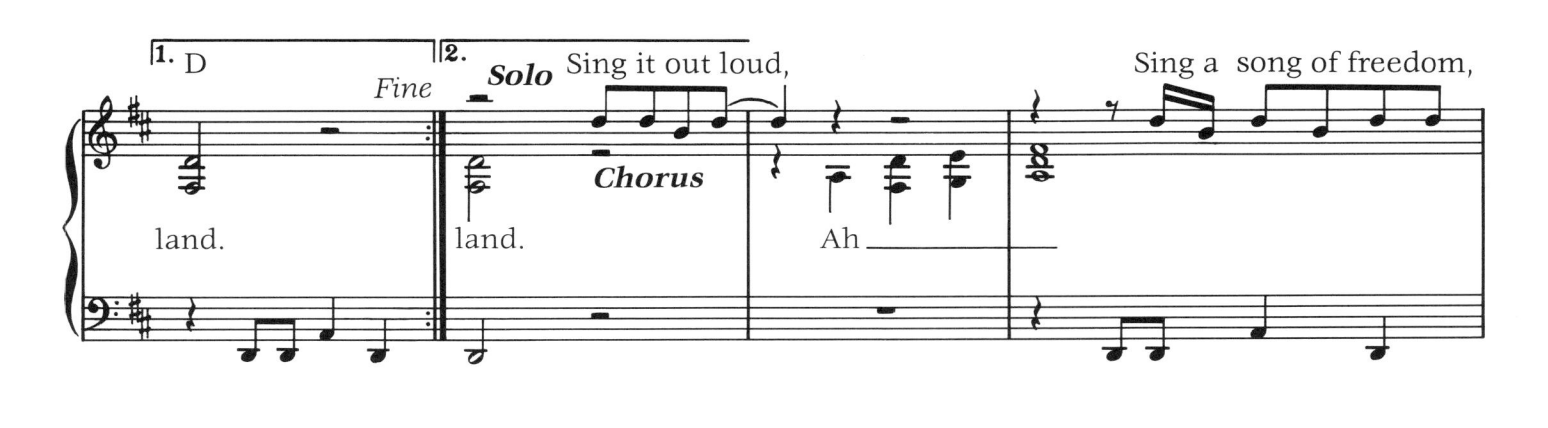

Rastafarianism

This religious movement grew up in the depressed areas of Jamaica in the 1930s, and during the 1950s grew rapidly in Britain among poorer blacks. Rastafarianism looks to Haile Selassie, former Emperor of Ethiopia, as the Black Messiah (*Ras Tafari*) and sees Western civilisation as 'Babylon', destined to be destroyed by God (Jah) on a day when black people will be repatriated in Africa (Zion).

Its beliefs are based on a selective but careful reading of the Bible, especially the Old Testament and the Book of Revelation. There is much biblical discussion (reasoning), and reggae music is much used.

This song 'Babylon' became popular in Britain and the first and third sections of it got into the charts. Omit the middle section if this is too difficult.

Songs of Praise

65 De angels rejoicin'

Traditional Caribbean

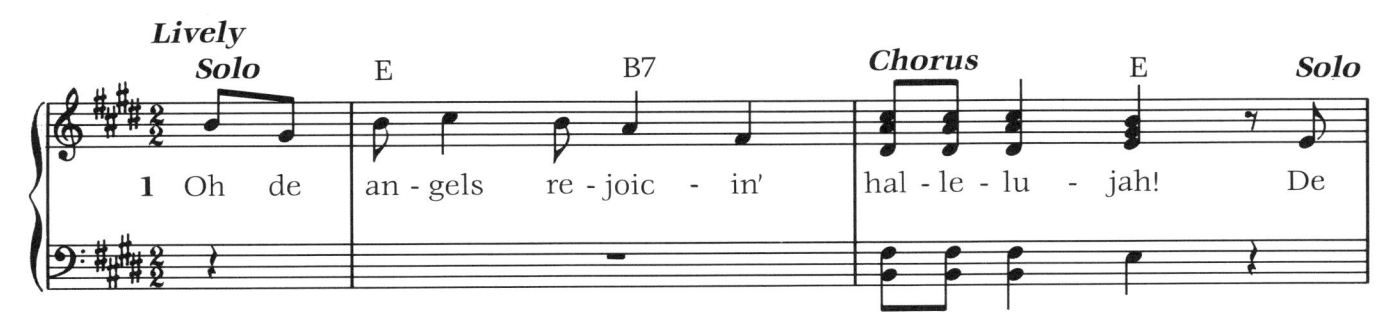

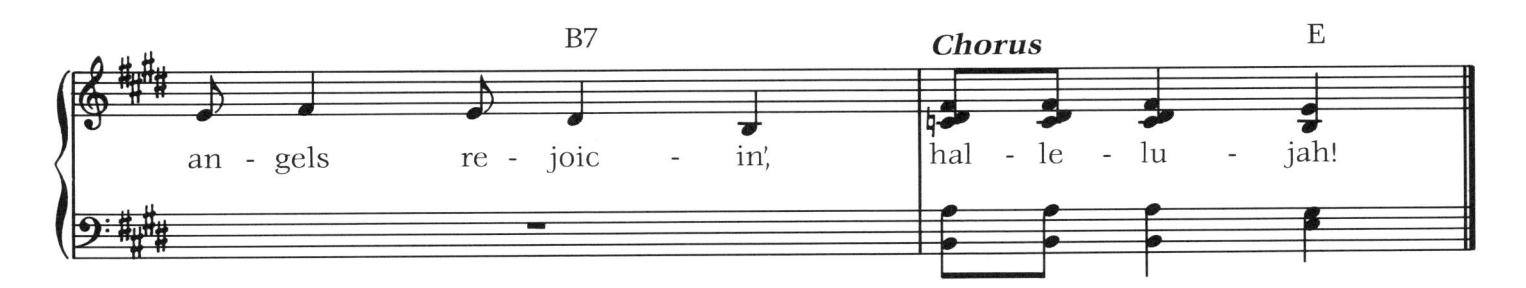

2 Now de heavens rejoicin', hallelujah,
   De angels rejoicin', hallelujah.

3 Had me hard, hard trials, hallelujah,
   De angels rejoicin', hallelujah.

4 Had me tribulations, hallelujah,
   Now de angels rejoicin', hallelujah.

5 All de stars rejoicin', hallelujah,
   De angels rejoicin', hallelujah.

6 Went away from religion, hallelujah,
   Now de angels rejoicin', hallelujah.

7 Now de heavens are openin', hallelujah,
   And de angels rejoicin', hallelujah.

8 Now de heavens rejoicin', hallelujah,
   'Cause de angels rejoicin', hallelujah.

Use the middle note of the right-hand part in the chorus sections as a simple alto part.

Pitched Percussion

A simpler version can use crotchets throughout.

Songs of Praise

66 A child's prayer

Urdu song by Allama Iqbal, collected from Habib Latif

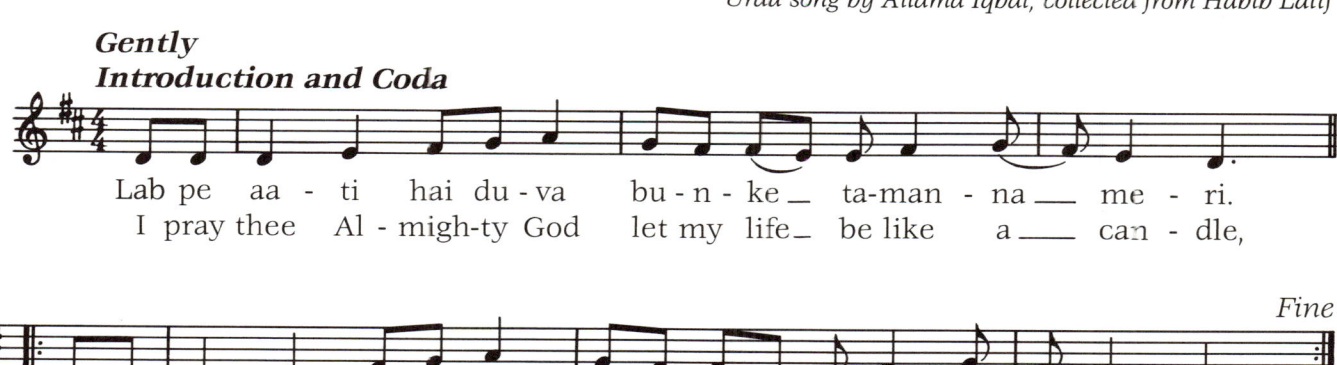

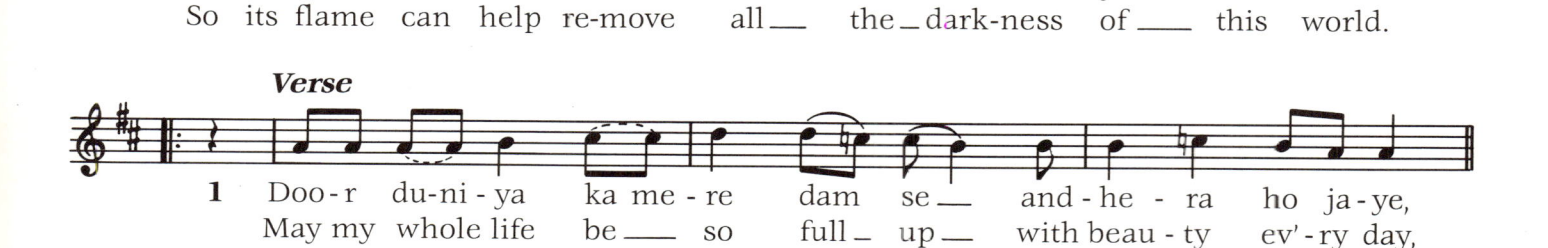

Gently
Introduction and Coda

Lab pe aa - ti hai du - va bu - n ke ta - man - na me - ri.
I pray thee Al - migh - ty God let my life be like a can - dle,

Fine

Zin - da - gi sha - ma ki su - ra t ho khu - da ya me - ri.
So its flame can help re - move all the dark - ness of this world.

Verse

1 Doo - r du - ni - ya ka me - re dam se and - he - ra ho ja - ye,
May my whole life be so full up with beau - ty ev' - ry day,

(Verse 5, repeat 3 times, then D.C. al Fine)

Har ja - ga me - ray cha - ma - k ne se u - ja - la ho ja - ye.
May my life spread its own beau - ty to light up the whole world.

2 Ho mere dum se yunhin meray watan ki zenat.
   Jis tarah phul se hoti hai chaman ki zenat. *(twice)*

3 Zindagi ho meray perwaney ki surat yarab.
   Ilm ki shama se ho mujhko muhabbat yarab. *(twice)*

Songs of Praise

4 Ho mera kam gharibon ki himayat karna.
   Dard-e-mando se zaifon se muhabbat karna. (*twice*)

5 Meray Allah burai se bachana mujhko.
   Nek jo raah ho usi rah pe chalana mujhko. (*three times*)
   Coda

*Some final consonants are sounded as separate syllables,
for example 'banke' = ban**u**ke ('u' as in **put**), 'surat' = surat**u**.*

2 May my whole life help to make my country heaven, like flowers
   Which enhance the beauty of the whole garden. (*twice*)

3 May my life be like a firefly which twinkles and flutters in the night.
   May I spend my life in love with the light of true knowledge. (*twice*)

4 May my whole life be given up to searching with great care
   For a way to end all injustice and all poverty. (*twice*)

5 Please God save me from ev'rything that's evil and bad
   And lead me forwards in the pathway of righteousness. (*three times*)
   Coda

This beautiful Muslim song shares with many traditions the search for beauty in life. It lends itself well to dramatisation.

Songs of Praise 123

67 The bell of creation

Sydney Carter

Gently
Introduction and Interlude

1 The bell of creation is swinging for ever In all of the things that are coming to be, The bell of creation is swinging for ever And all of the while it is swinging in me.

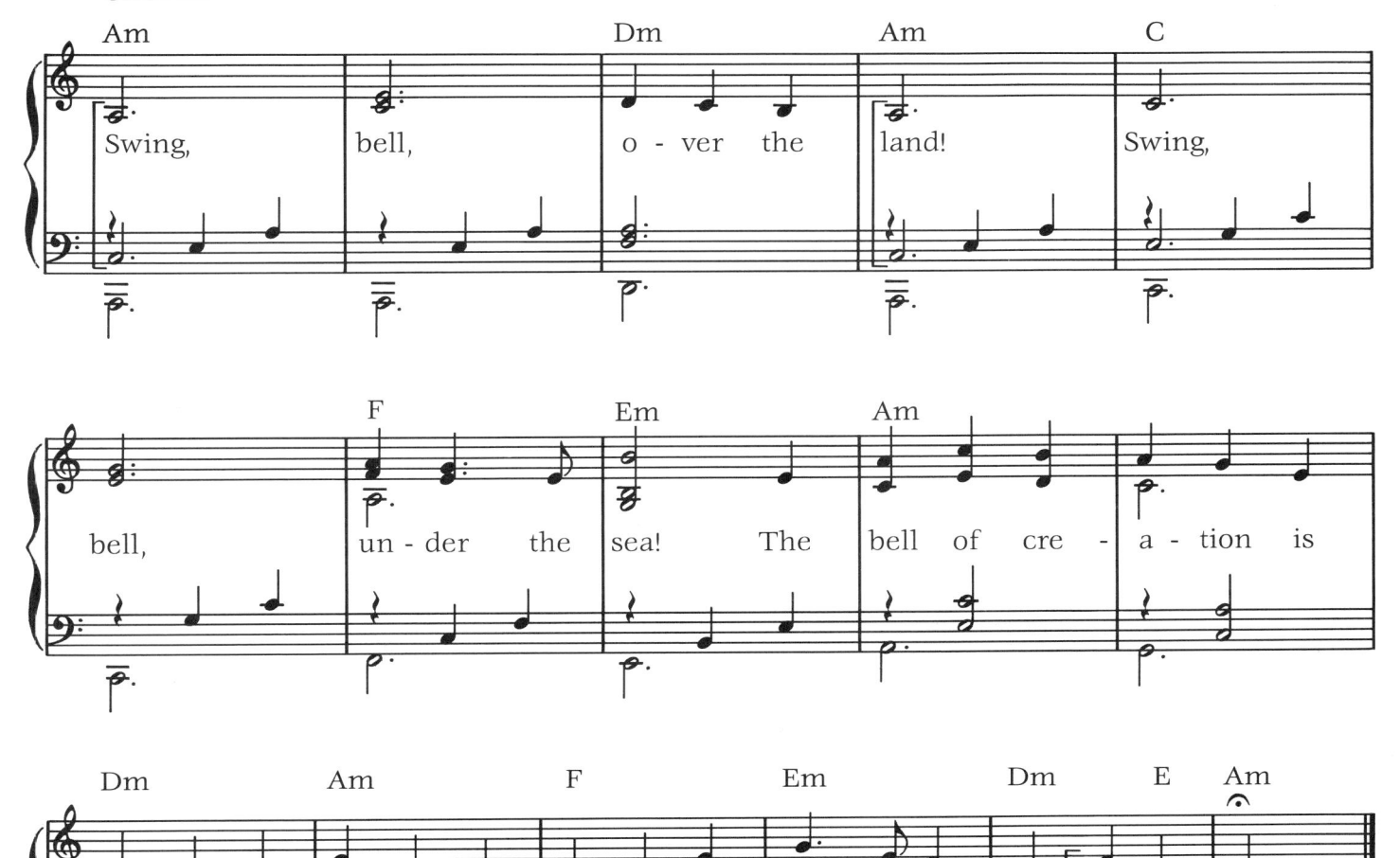

Chorus

Swing, bell, o-ver the land! Swing, bell, un-der the sea! The bell of cre-a-tion is swing-ing for e-ver And all of the while it is swing-ing in me.

2 In all of my loving, in all of my labour,
   In all of the things that are coming to be,
   In all of my loving, in all of my labour,
   The bell of creation is swinging in me.
   Chorus

3 I look for the life that is living for ever
   In all of the things that are coming to be,
   I look for the life that is living for ever
   And all of the while it is looking for me.
   Chorus

4 I'll swing with the bell that is swinging for ever
   In all of the things that are coming to be,
   I'll swing with the bell that is swinging for ever
   And all of the while it is swinging in me.
   Chorus

Songs of Praise

Pitched Percussion

Chorus

This popular song by Sydney Carter sees the creative potential in everyone.

Index of song titles

A child's prayer	122
A happy time	20
A jari for harvest	12
Allah ju main	79
A Lyke Wake dirge	80
Apples and honey	8
Arabic wedding chant	78
Are bhalo	12
Arnaki ke likos	44
Avare varsad	60
Aye re aye	60
Bless our country	88
Buddha Lord we offer	58
Buddhist blessings	90
By the rivers of Babylon	118
Cân y grempog	38
Carol of the creatures	116
Charni may bahar	26
Cheshire souling song	18
Chinese lantern song	34
Chinese New Year	32
Come, come, rain	60
Come, let us go	70
De angels rejoicin'	121
Eid is here	60
Eid ul-Bukr	62
Farewell song	71
Gandhi's favourite hymn	97
Great is His love	39
Hare Krishna	114
Hevenu Shalom	96
Hey Motswala	76
Holi with Shyam	50
Holy day of Wesak	58
Hoya-hoye	68
H'ristos anesti	46
I am all alone	79
I'm building a sukkah	10
Initiation song	74
Into the future	98
Jabbin, Jabbin	65
Jon, jané, jana	100
Japanese New Year's song	30
Jesus has risen	46
Jesus's birth	24
John Barleycorn	56
Joy in the manger	26
Kalo sile	70
Koee bolay Ram Ram	102
Let us praise Him	115
Like a beautiful journey	92
Lord of all hopefulness	64
Lord Ram	113
Love your neighbour	87
Master Hee-haw	28
Matsukazari	30
Munji Aziz ka jnumdin	24
My name is Purim	36
Nkosi sikelel'i Afrika	88
Ogun ba mi re	107
Oh Chanukah	22
On the first Thanksgiving Day	16
One world	82
Onisango	108
Padstow May Day song	54
Peace unto you	96
Phagun lege	52
Praise Lord Krishna	114
Raghupati	97
Rise! Rise!	65
Ruaumoko	109
Ruu tat	106
Salani	71
Sanctus	105
Shabbat shalom	66
Shri Ram	113
Simple gifts	94
Somagwaza	74
Some do call you Rama	102
Song to Ogun	107
Spring song	52
Still now	72
Tapuchim ud' vash	8
The bell of creation	124
The heavens are speaking	106
The lamb and the wolf	44
The pancake song	38
The Son of God	48
The world is dark	84
Twameva	112
Village festival	15
We'll come again	68
Whey he day?	42
You are my mother	112
ɔdɔ N'eye	87

Index of first lines (in English)

A happy time is Diwali	20
All the birds are calling, Rise!	65
Apples and honey for Rosh Hashanah	8
As I stood beneath the sky	106
Bless, O Lord, our country Africa	88
Buddha Lord we offer	58
By the rivers of Babylon	118
Come, come, rain	60
Come let's celebrate Jesus' birthday today	24
Come, let us go, come, let us go into your house	70
Creator high and holy	116
Down at our village shrine see flowers bright we lay	15
Eid is here, Eid is here	60
Eid ul-Bukr, It's a happy festive day	62
Farewell now, may you farewell	71
From the East and long ago	28
Happy New Year to you!	32
I am all alone, O God	79
I pray thee Almighty God let my life be like a candle	122
I'm building a sukkah	10
Is all well with you, brother?	12
It's the springs up in the mountains make the rivers of the plain	82
King Ram of the Rhagu family	97
Lady of this big, fine house	38
Let's go and see the lanterns today	34
Let us praise Him	115
Like a beautiful journey is life	92
Look how He is lying in a manger	26
Lord of all hopefulness, Lord of all joy	64
Lord Ram, praise Ram, praise, praise Ram	113
My mamma travelled to Pretoria	76
My mother you are and my father you are	112
My name is Purim and I come	36
Next year on this day, we'll come again	68
O all people on the earth, love your neighbour as yourself	87
O give thanks to the Lord for He is good	39
Oh Chanukah, Oh Chanukah, come light the menorah	22
Oh de angels rejoicin'	121
Oh Jesus has risen from the dead	46
On the eve of New Year's	30
On the first Thanksgiving Day	16
On this day let's play Holi with Shyam	50
Once there was a little lamb	44
Praise Lord Krishna	114
See how the spring is coming now in woods and fields!	52
Set out in the cool of the morning	98
Some do call you Rama, and others Khuda	102
Still now and hear my singing	72
The bell of creation is swinging for ever	124
The lightning strikes!	109
The Master called and I replied	100
The Son of God gave His life for us	48
The world is dark, we need the light	84
There came three men from out of the west	56
This ae nicht, this ae night	80
'Tis the gift to be simple, 'tis the gift to be free	94
To forsake the foolish and follow the wise	90
Unite and unite and let us all unite	54
Whey he day?	42
You gentlemen of England	18